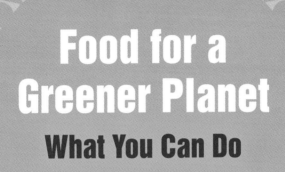

Food for a Greener Planet

What You Can Do

GREEN ISSUES IN FOCUS

Lisa A. Wroble

Enslow Publishers, Inc.
40 Industrial Road
Box 398
Berkeley Heights, NJ 07922
USA
http://www.enslow.com

Library of Congress Cataloging-in-Publication Data

Wroble, Lisa A.
  Food for a greener planet : what you can do / Lisa A. Wroble.
    p. cm. — (Green issues in focus)
  Includes bibliographical references and index.
  Summary:"Read about how food goes from field to fork, how food is grown, problems with farming techniques, and sustainable farming"—Provided by publisher.
  ISBN 978-0-7660-3349-8
  1. Food—Environmental aspects—Juvenile literature. 2. Sustainable agriculture—Juvenile literature. I. Title.
  TX355.W76 2011
  641.3—dc22
                                    2010022077
Printed in the United States of America

082010 Lake Book Manufacturing, Inc., Melrose Park, IL

10 9 8 7 6 5 4 3 2 1

To Our Readers: We have done our best to make sure all Internet Addresses in this book were active and appropriate when we went to press. However, the author and the publisher have no control over and assume no liability for the material available on those Internet sites or on other Web sites they may link to. Any comments or suggestions can be sent by e-mail to comments@enslow.com or to the address on the back cover. Every effort has been made to locate all copyright holders of material used in this book. If any errors or omissions have occurred, corrections will be made in future editions.

♻ Enslow Publishers, Inc., is committed to printing our books on recycled paper. The paper in every book contains 10% to 30% post-consumer waste (PCW). The cover board on the outside of each book contains 100% PCW. Our goal is to do our part to help young people and the environment too!

Illustration Credits: Associated Press, p. 85; Stephen Ausmus/Agricultural Research Service, U.S. Department of Agriculture (ARS-USDA), pp. 42, 101; Rhoda Baer/National Cancer Institute, p. 91; Scott Bauer/ARS-USDA, pp. 4, 33, 61, 99; Jack Dykinga/ARS-USDA, pp. 69, 103; Yue Jin/ARS-USDA, p. 50; Bob Nicols/ARS-USDA, p. 80; Photos.com, pp. 22, 100; Shutterstock. com, pp. 3, 11, 14, 37, 70, 71, 95, 96, 99, 105; Kay Simmons/ARS-USDA, pp. 53, 102; USDA National Agricultural Library, Food and Nutrition Service, pp. 26, 47; U.S. Food and Drug Administration, p. 30, Keith Weller/ARS-USDA, pp. 77, 104.

Cover Illustration: Shutterstock.com.

Contents

Teens Choosing "Green" Food

"I love my vegetables," says Michelle Simpson, a senior at Heritage High School in Baltimore, Maryland. She proudly shows visitors to Hoop Village the kale and cabbage she helped plant. Hoop Village is an urban-farming program that uses three plastic-covered greenhouses to teach skills in agriculture, horticulture, and marketing. In addition to providing "green" jobs, students market their produce to the northeast Baltimore community.[1]

Throughout the United States teens are learning about growing food. Many programs sell the harvest to local markets, restaurants, and their own school cafeterias. In the process, they learn that "green" food is more than the color of vegetables such as broccoli, spinach, kale, and leafy greens.

"Green" food is a term used to mean the way food is grown or raised—without chemicals, and in a way that is good for the earth. It also means how animals are raised for meat. Standard farming uses chemicals. These chemicals get rid of pests. They make food and animals grow faster.

Chemicals are also used to treat the soil. They help refresh the soil. In the past, manure did this job. Standard farming has become like a huge company. It keeps trying to find faster ways to produce more. Seeds and plants are altered to make this happen. Livestock is bred to a certain size and body shape. This allows the machines that butcher the meat to work faster.

"Green" food is often used to mean organic farming. Organic farming is natural farming. It returns to traditional ways of raising crops. Food is grown without chemicals. A variety of crops are planted, not just those that grow faster or are in demand. Animals are raised with patience. They graze outside the barn. When ready, they are butchered based on their own size and shape.

These are two types of farming—traditional, organic farming, and standard, factory farms. In the gap between these two extremes exists the true sense of what "green" food means. Green food also means sustainable agriculture.

Sustainable agriculture is a type of farming. It makes sure the land used to grow food will be healthy and able to grow different foods for many, many generations. Sustainable farming asks that we become stewards of the land. This means we take care not to pollute soil, air, or water. It asks that we understand how soil, air, water, and sunlight work together for food to be grown and livestock to be raised.

"Green" food, then, is concerned with the cycle of food from farm to table. How food is grown or raised, shipped, packaged, and made ready for sale are all factors for whether food is "green" or not.

Food is important. Our bodies need food for survival. But the type and quality of that food does make a difference. This is where green food comes into the picture. Chemicals used to grow, ripen, process, and preserve food is just one issue related to green food. Green food honors sustainable farming so the soil and farms are still able to grow enough food to feed people years from now. It considers how to limit chemicals. These chemicals may end up harming the water and air, or even those who eat the food. Green food farming tries to provide more choices for fresh, whole foods to all people, whether they live in the country or city, and whether they are rich or poor.

1

Food, Glorious Food

Hungry? Look around. Options for feeding that hunger are everywhere. Hot pretzels and popcorn tempt us at the mall. Ice cream and hot dogs are available on the street corner. Vending machines willingly dump out candy and snacks at the drop of several coins. Convenience stores are stocked with chips, cookies, snack foods, soda, chocolate milk, and other temptations.

For something more filling, head to the nearest deli, pizza parlor, sub shop, or fast-food restaurant. Of course, you can also go to the grocery store for frozen food ready to microwave.

These options all focus on quickly filling an empty stomach. If you have time, making a meal at home from groceries bought at the store may sound better.

Overwhelmed With Food

In North America we are surrounded by food. Nine out of ten TV ads on Saturday mornings feature sugary, high fat food, according to a study requested by the Centers for Disease Control and Prevention (CDC).[1] We are a population who eats meals on the go. We eat snacks often. Protein bars and energy drinks help us hold out until dinnertime. And then, of course, we cannot forget our nighttime snacks in front of the computer or TV before bed.

Defining Overweight

What is the difference between being overweight and obese? It relates to the amount of body fat in relation to height and weight. Calculating a body mass index (BMI) provides a percentile rank. In the United States, BMI charts are created by the Centers for Disease Control and Prevention (CDC). For children and teens, a BMI-for-age is used. It factors in age and gender since the amount of body fat changes as children grow. A rank between the 5th and 85th percentile is a healthy weight. A percentile between 85 and 95 is considered overweight, while a percentile above 95 is considered obese.[2]

Despite the abundance of food most North Americans enjoy, we are experiencing a food crisis. Instead of being healthy, many of us are overweight. In the United States, 17 percent of young people aged twelve to nineteen are considered overweight.[3] In Canada, obesity rates have tripled over twenty years. Twenty-six percent of Canadian youth aged two to seventeen are considered overweight or obese.[4]

It comes down to food choices. Fast and prepackaged foods are convenient. But they pile on the calories. They may help us feel full but they lack some key nutrients. It is the type of food we consume that creates the problem.

How the Body Uses Food

The food we eat is a mix of thousands of compounds. Our body actually uses only the nutrients in whatever we eat. The body breaks down the food to get at the nutrients it needs. This is called digestion. It begins in the mouth where saliva breaks down carbohydrates such as grains and starches. It continues in the stomach and small intestines. Gastric juices break down what we have eaten. Carbohydrates become simple sugars. Proteins are broken down into amino acids. Fats are broken down into fatty acids. The body absorbs the nutrients through the walls of the intestines. Whatever is left leaves the body as waste.

While these foods may make you feel full, they are not the healthiest options.

Nutrients are grouped into six categories. We need some of these nutrients in large amounts. These are called *macronutrients*. Carbohydrates, protein, water, and fat are the nutrients we need most. We need two types of nutrients in smaller amounts. These are called *micronutrients*. They are the vitamins and minerals found in foods we eat.

The body needs nutrients for three functions. Nutrients provide energy, growth, and continued health. Nutrients in food provide fuel for energy. The body first burns the sugars from carbohydrates. This allows energy for moving, thinking, even breathing. In addition, it gives the body energy to use the other nutrients. Amino acids and fatty acids are used to build or repair body cells and tissues. They also help maintain body systems and keep the whole body running smoothly. If the body needs to, it can also burn fatty acids for energy. Extra nutrients, such as fats or proteins, are stored by the body to use later. The body stores them as fat. So, if we eat more than we need to, those extra calories are also stored as fat.[5]

When people do not get enough to eat, they become undernourished. This means their bodies are starved for nutrients. They are not getting the protein, fats, carbohydrates, vitamins, or minerals needed to live. Severe undernourishment is called malnutrition. Food programs in poor countries, such as those in Africa, try to prevent hunger. Such hunger can lead to malnutrition. Even people who are not starving in these countries may not get enough nutrition. Lack of needed nutrients can cause illness. When the body is weakened, it cannot protect itself from disease.

This balance of eating and getting the right nutrients is important for every living thing. If a plant does not get what it needs from the soil, it will grow, but it may not be healthy. The animals we eat for meat also eat plants for food. If the plants are not healthy, animals will not be healthy. If both the plants and meat we eat

You Can: Focus on Fresh Food

Put down the candy bars, chips, and cookies. Check the wrappers. How many of the ingredients are hard to pronounce? These foods, which are ready to eat, are called prepackaged. They are highly processed. Refined flour, sugar, flavorings, and preservatives add up to yummy tastes. But how much of it is your body able to use?

Instead of reaching for prepackaged food as a snack, try fresh food. Vegetables, fruits, and nuts are just as easy to eat on the go. Bananas even come in their own natural packaging.

Fresh food is whole food. It is not made in a factory. It is not processed into "food products." It does not have refined sugar or flour added. According to food writer Cheryl Redmond, "Whole fruits and vegetables offer vitamins in a form your body uses best." She explains that even vitamin makers have not been able to copy "the way nature's bounty preserves and delivers these nutrients."[6]

When fresh food is not available, dried fruits are good snacking choices. They are processed, but not like cakes, cookies, chips, candy, and snack foods. The processing dries the fruit. Sometimes a preservative is added. But you will be able to read and pronounce the ingredients on these packages.

Some teens may have a hard time finding fresh, whole food. In large cities, the produce section at the grocery store may be meager. In low-income areas, the cost of fresh fruit and vegetables can be high. And organic fruit and vegetables can be even more expensive.

Farmers' markets bring fresh, whole food from nearby farms to cities and towns. Find local markets in a city near you at Local Harvest. Another option is a food cooperative, or co-op. Members work together to run a store, market, or farm. They receive some of the products or harvest for their work. New programs are bringing fresh food to inner cities. One, started by activist Zena Nelson, is called the South Bronx Food Cooperative. This green market stocks healthy, organic, and free-trade foods and eco-friendly cleaning supplies at half the cost of other stores, says food writer Katie Arnold.[7]

The fruits and vegetables in the produce section are some of the most natural foods found in a grocery store.

do not get the nutrients they need, our bodies will not get the nutrients they need.

You Are What You Eat

All living things need food. Green plants use sunlight to make food. The sun gives plants energy. This energy helps plants turn water and minerals from the soil and carbon dioxide, a gas from the air, into food. The food allows plants to grow. People and animals use the food made by plants for energy. People get food from plants. Most people also get food by eating animals. Those animals ate plants for food. If the animals eat poor quality food, they will not provide the best nutrients for us.

Basic foods we get from plants are grains, vegetables, and fruits. Animals provide meat, eggs, and milk. For variety, people combine these basic foods to create other foods. Milk is turned into cheese or yogurt. Grains are made into bread or cereal. The most common grains in North America are corn, wheat, and rice.

In developing countries, such as those in Africa, the main foods come from plants, including grain. Meat or food from animals makes up a greater part of the diet in developed countries, such as the United States. Though many foods, such as eggs, fruits, and vegetables are sold in their whole, natural form, animals are butchered into cuts of meat for the market. The meat is then cooked. Herbs, mushrooms, and spices are added to meat and other cooked dishes. They add flavor and variety.

When fruits and vegetables are picked and eaten, it is called fresh, whole food. When vegetables, herbs, and meat are cooked together, it is called simple food. Both types of food are very close to the way nature gave them to us. They are filled with nutrients. Once food is picked, though, it loses very tiny amounts of nutrients. So, as it sits waiting to be eaten, more and more nutrients leach away. Meat must be kept cold after it is

Hidden Hunger

Even when people have more than enough to eat, they can become unhealthy. Many Americans have plenty of food, but poor health. They eat the wrong kinds of foods. Or the food they eat does not include enough nutrients. Nutrients are needed to maintain body systems. They keep the whole body healthy. So, both undernourishment and malnutrition can happen even when people have plenty to eat. According to the Food and Agriculture Organization of the United Nations, *both* undernutrition and obesity are now problems in developing countries.[8]

Obesity can happen when we eat foods with too many of the wrong nutrients, such as carbohydrates and fats. The body does not need them, so they are stored. Meanwhile, the body suffers because it still needs vitamins, minerals, or protein. The body sends signals that nutrients are needed. So people keep eating, but unless they eat the right foods, their bodies will still need certain vitamins and minerals. But they are still not the right foods. The body starves for what it needs, yet plenty of food is available.

Jim Goodman, organic farmer in Wisconsin and policy board member of Organic Consumers Association, blames the way food is grown. "According to the USDA," he says, "Americans are increasingly deficient in calcium, potassium, magnesium, and vitamins A, C, D, and E." He explains that the lower levels of vitamins, minerals, and other nutrients in the foods we eat mean the soil on farms is depleted. This means the soil is worn out. If the soil does not have enough of the right nutrients for the plants to be healthy, the food from the plants will not have enough of the nutrients our bodies need. Goodman says this poor soil quality is "caused by industrial farming practices."[9]

butchered. It must also be cooked soon after, or it will spoil.

The more that is done to food to make it ready for us to eat, the less nutritious it can become. This is why it is important to understand where food comes from—to know how food is grown, picked, and shipped. It is also important to know how some food is packaged and processed before it reaches the market.

Convenience vs. Nutrition

Much of the food from farms goes to food-packaging plants. Some is packaged whole to ship to stores and markets. Most is turned into ready-to-eat or quick-to-make foods. The steps taken to do this is called food processing. This change from fresh food to ready-to-eat food products changes the quality of the food we eat most often during the day.

Look down the aisles at any supermarket. They are filled with canned, dried, and frozen foods. These foods are all prepared at food-packing plants. Some foods are processed. This means they are combined to make new foods. For example, canned soup, pasta sauce, and baked goods such as bread, cakes, and muffins. Refined sugar, flour, salt, and preservatives are often added during processing. The preservatives allow these foods to last longer on the shelf without spoiling. Food-packing plants also make frozen dinners, microwave meals, and mix-and-eat instant-food products. These are all called convenience foods. They make it easy to fix a meal or a snack. If they are not ready to open and eat, they are fast to make and eat.

These foods might taste yummy to some individuals. Especially when compared to snacking on vegetables. But remember that the body needs certain nutrients to be healthy. Our bodies only use the nutrients in the food we eat. Whole, fresh foods are loaded with nutrients our bodies can use. They do not contain additives our bodies do not need. This is why whole, fresh food is the best food choice. Healthy food fortifies the body. "Plant cells offer the perfect protective environment for vitamins, minerals, and phytochemicals like flavonoids," explains food writer Cheryl Redmond. Plant cells keep these nutrients protected. They will stay powerful and give the body plenty to use to stay healthy.[10] Eating fresh, whole food helps fight disease. It may even slow down aging because antioxidants in plant foods keep our skin cells healthy.

From Field to Fork

Where does food come from? The grocery store or market, of course. But how does it get there? Perhaps you have noticed signs near fruits or vegetables in the store or on labels on the foods themselves: "Product of Mexico" or "Grown in Brazil." That is a long way to travel. How does it get from the field to our table?

All food is grown or raised. Vegetables and grains, such as oats and wheat, are grown on farms. Fruits and most nuts are grown in orchards or groves. These are farms with acres of trees of the same type—an orchard of apple trees, for instance, or a citrus grove with sections for orange, lemon, lime, and grapefruit trees.

Meat is raised on farms, too. Sometimes these farms are called ranches. Beef comes from cattle raised on cattle ranches. Pork comes from hogs. When the animals are grown, they are sent to a slaughterhouse. Here the meat is cut and sent to markets and butcher shops.

A poultry farm raises hens for eggs and meat. A dairy farm raises cows for milk. The milk is sold to a dairy plant., which bottles milk and makes cheese and yogurt.

When the food is ripe it is picked. This is called harvesting. It is called raw or whole food. Some raw food is shipped to stores. Shoppers call it fresh food.

Food-Packing Plants

Most whole, fresh food is sold to food plants— companies that make the food ready to eat. Eggs are packed in cartons. Milk is made into cheese. Beef and pork are made into lunch meat. Grain is ground into flour. Even sugar needs to be made. It is refined from sugar beets or sugarcane to make white sugar. These foods are all made or prepared in food plants. Then it is packaged and shipped to stores.

Some of these foods are used to make other food. Snack cakes and muffins use eggs, flour, and refined sugar. These are called processed foods. We open the package and eat them. For example, breakfast bars, cookies, muffins, and snack cakes are ready to eat out of the package. To eat other foods, a little preparation is needed. For example, we might open a loaf of bread and lunch meat to make a sandwich, or open a box of cereal and a bottle of milk to make a quick breakfast. Some processed foods need to be heated and then served. Frozen dinners, a can of soup, or hot dogs are examples.

Packaged foods are also called convenience foods. Without them we would have a lot of work to do before we could eat. For example, to make a peanut butter and jelly sandwich you would have to bake bread; then grind peanuts into peanut butter; and then wash, peel, mash, and cook fruit into jelly. Of course, you would have enough for many sandwiches. But when all of these foods are made for us, they make life easier.

Meatpacking Plants

Processing makes meat safer to eat. Animals raised for meat are sent to a butcher shop or slaughterhouse. A butcher usually handles only a few animals at a time. A slaughterhouse handles many. According to investigative writer Eric Schlosser, "Twenty years ago, new meatpacking plants in the High Plains slaughtered about 175 cattle an hour." Today faster equipment allows them to slaughter 400 cattle an hour.[1] Meatpacking plants are very large slaughterhouses, often owned by companies that raise the animals. For example, Smithfield Foods, one of the largest pork producers, owns 1.2 million sows., which give birth to the pigs raised for food. The company also slaughters the pigs and packages pork products sold in grocery stores.[2]

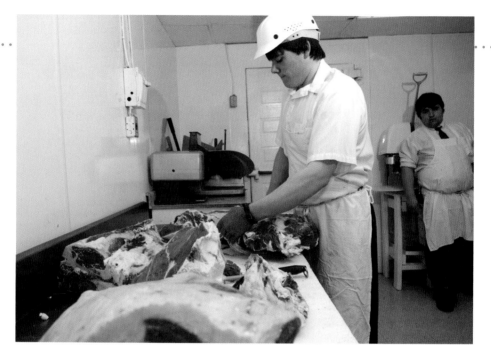

Beef is trimmed and sliced into different cuts of meat before being sold to restaurants and grocery stores.

Whether the company is large or small, the animal is first killed. Then a carcass is prepared. The parts of the animal that we do not eat, such as the gut, organs, skin, head, and legs, are removed. If this is not done properly, the meat will get spoiled. For example, animal feces from the gut could pollute the meat.[3]

Then the carcass is divided into sections. These sections are trimmed and cut into different cuts of meat. Like produce from a farm, some meat is sent to food-packaging plants, where it is processed into ready-to-eat food. Some meat is sent to stores. The butcher at the store cuts the meat into smaller portions. Some is ground to make hamburgers or sausage. Without people to cut meat and make it ready to eat, we would have to do this work before we could cook the meat.

Food Additives

When fresh foods are blended to make new foods, such as sausage, bread, or muffins, salt and spices are added. These improve the flavor. Food-packing plants also add other ingredients. They are called food additives. These make the food look and taste better. Some are also added to help hold the food together—so muffins are not too crumbly, or so oil in peanut butter does not separate as it sits on a shelf.

The Food and Drug Administration (FDA) regulates food additives. According to the FDA Web site, "Additives have been used for many years to preserve, flavor, blend, thicken and color foods."[4] Additives allow food to be stored long past harvest. They keep the food fresh and make it more appealing. Cooking food sometimes makes it lose color. Food dyes are added to change the coloring so we will want to eat it.

Color is not the only thing lost when food is cooked. Cooking food changes the texture and nutrients are sometimes lost. According to the *USDA Table of Nutrient*

Retention Factors, how much of the nutrients are lost depends on how the food is cooked. Higher temperatures often leach more nutrients. Yet freezing retains up to 95 percent of the nutrients.[5] Boiling vegetables, for example, releases water-soluble vitamins, which are then lost when the water is drained before serving. So additives are used to replace lost nutrients during food processing. Sometimes additives are used to boost the nutrients in foods to make them healthier. Energy bars are one example.

Chemicals in Food

Read the list of ingredients on food you eat. Most of the words are hard to pronounce. They sound like chemicals from a laboratory. For this reason, people sometimes assume that food additives are chemicals and that adding chemicals to food must be harmful. In truth, all foods are made up of chemicals. An orange plucked from a tree contains ascorbic acid, which is also called vitamin C. Ascorbic acid may be added to foods to boost nutrition or to delay spoiling. This additive may come from oranges. Or it may be made in a laboratory. Both are identical.

Like that orange, food that is grown and animals raised for meat contain chemicals. The food safety Web site of the FDA says that every living thing is made "of the chemical building blocks of carbon, hydrogen,

Who Makes Sure Food is Safe?

The Food and Drug Administration (FDA) is part of the federal government. This agency protects public health by checking that food, cosmetics, and drugs for humans and animals are not harmful. It approves what can be added to food during processing and inspects food-packaging plants.

The FDA notifies the public when something may cause illness or injury. For example, if something made at a specific packaging plant causes food poisoning, the FDA looks into it. It issues recalls. The product is pulled from store shelves. News announcements alert people that they should not eat or use a recalled product.

The FDA is not responsible for inspecting restaurants. Meat and poultry are inspected by the U.S. Department of Agriculture (USDA). The FDA, USDA, and Environmental Protection Agency (EPA) share the obligation for chemicals used on crops.[6]

nitrogen, oxygen, and other elements."[7] These combine to make proteins, fats, starches, water, and vitamins, which are in our bodies and in foods we eat.

Concern over chemicals in foods is linked with preservatives, chemicals added to keep food from spoiling. Preservatives are important. Much of the shelf stable food we buy does not need to be stored in the refrigerator. Once the food is opened it will spoil. This

Many shoppers carefully read labels so that they know what is in the food that they are eating.

is when we need to store it in the refrigerator. These packaged foods use preservatives so they can stay on store shelves longer.

There are two types of preservatives added to food. One type is antimicrobial. These keep mold, yeast, and bacteria from growing. The other type is antioxidant. These curb the reaction between air, light, and heat with the food. They keep the food from turning brown or rancid. They also protect essential amino acids in food. Amino acids are the building blocks of proteins.[8]

Foods that come ready to open, heat, and eat, such as TV dinners or frozen pizzas, go through more preparation. Many ingredients are processed and then combined to create the meal. For example, for the frozen pizza, dough and sauce are made, then the cheese, meat, and vegetable toppings are prepared. These meals are known as heavily processed foods. They often contain more preservatives than foods used to cook a meal at home.

Preserving Food

Adding chemicals to food is not the only way to keep it fresh. Different methods are also used. Many have been used for centuries. Salting meat was used by ancient Egyptians.[9] Ancient Egyptians also dried fruit, beans, and fish to store for later use.[10] Some foods we enjoy today were early ways to store food. Pickling is an example. Vegetables, meat, or fish are soaked in saltwater brine for many days. They are drained and then stored in vinegar. The most popular item is pickled cucumbers, or "pickles." Cheese is another example. Enzymes added to milk changed the taste and texture. And cheese lasts much longer than the milk it is made from.

All food contains natural enzymes. These are proteins that ripen or age food. Once food is picked, the enzymes break down, and the food begins to spoil. When food is left on the kitchen counter, bacteria and microorganisms also cause spoilage.[11] Washing the skins of vegetables and fruits removes some bacteria. Placing food in the refrigerator slows the bacteria and enzymes down. Food does not spoil as quickly. Freezing stops the process. The enzymes and bacteria become inactive. When the food is thawed and opened, the process begins again.

Another way to stop bacteria is to sterilize food. Boiling or heating food to high temperatures kills bacteria. Canning uses this process. Food is placed in jars or cans, which are sealed with lids and then heated. As the food inside is sterilized, the container seals. The bacteria are killed. The seal keeps new bacteria out. Canned food can be stored on the shelf for a long time. Once it is opened, though, bacteria can get in. This is why opened cans and jars are stored in the refrigerator.

Cans and jars are not the only containers used for canning food today. Foil pouches of tuna, plastic cups of fruit, and boxes of juice are all "canned." Juice and milk found in boxes on grocery store shelves use a special canning method. Ultra high temperature (UHT) pasteurization kills bacteria using a very high temperature for two seconds.[12] Because the beverage is sterilized and sealed, it does not need to be refrigerated.

Most milk is pasteurized. All milk contains natural bacteria. Left at room temperature, it spoils within several hours. Refrigerating helps. But it still spoils in a day. Boiling milk to sterilize it changes the taste. Pasteurization does not change the taste. The milk is heated to a temperature high enough to kill some of the bacteria and stop the enzymes. The milk can be stored in the refrigerator for about a week.

Drying food also prevents spoilage. Dried food is called dehydrated. The water is removed. Dried food can be stored in airtight containers for a very long time. The texture and taste of the food is changed. But new foods are the result. Raisins are dried grapes. Prunes are dried plums. Drying brings out the natural sugar in fruits so they taste sweeter than fresh fruit.

Freeze-drying is another way to dehydrate food. The taste does not change as much as in drying. In freeze-drying, food is frozen then placed in a strong vacuum. Water in the food freezes. The vacuum causes it to change from ice into vapor. The water or liquid stage is skipped. Instant coffee is made through freeze-drying.

A less common method is irradiation. It uses nuclear radiation to kill almost all the bacteria. It does not sterilize the food, though. Food can be sealed in a plastic and irradiated. Since it is sealed, new bacteria cannot get in, so the package is safe to store on a shelf. This method does not change the flavor or texture of food. Thirty-seven countries, including the United States, have deemed irradiation safe for forty different foods, according to food safety specialist Charlotte P.

You Can: Understand Food Labels

Our bodies use only the nutrients in food. They get rid of the rest. When the food we eat has a lot of preservatives, food dyes, and artificial ingredients, our bodies cannot use them. Reading food labels will help you understand what nutrition your body is getting. Begin with the list of ingredients. They are listed in quantity order by weight. For example, "flour" is listed first in bread, cakes, and muffins. Where on the list are additives listed? They are listed at the end because they are used in small amounts.

	% Daily Value*
Total Fat 12g	18%
Saturated Fat 3g	15%
Trans Fat 3g	
Cholesterol 30mg	10%
Sodium 470mg	20%
Total Carbohydrate 31g	10%

Ingredients: Enriched flour (flour, malted barley, niacin, reduced iron, thiamin mononitrate, riboflavin, folic acid), sugar, partially hydrogenated cottonseed oil, high fructose corn syrup, whey, eggs, vanilla, natural and artificial flavoring, salt, leavening (sodium acid pyrophosphate, monocalcium phosphate), lecithin, mono- and diglycerides.

Brennand, PhD.[13] The FDA has approved it for many different foods, including wheat, fruit, vegetables, potatoes, flour, spices, chicken, pork, and beef. According to writer Marshall Brain, "Many people have a significant problem with the words 'nuclear radiation.'"[14] It is used most frequently in food preparation for the military, in institutions such as hospitals, and on dried spices.

All these ways of packaging food and keeping it fresh allow us to have plenty of food all year. We have many choices in the foods we buy. Fresh vegetables and fruits can be eaten raw. Or they can be blended with meat or grain to make a meal. Packaged food allows us to make a meal with little effort. If time is short, a frozen dinner is ready in minutes using a microwave.

Many of these options were not available twenty years ago. Once, farms grew food for the people living only in cities nearby. People knew where their food came from. They ate what was available during specific months of the year. Farmland disappeared as cities grew bigger. Farmers had to feed more people. More food was preserved and packaged so it could be eaten long after it was grown. The plants that made these foods needed raw food from farmers. Farmers had to increase crops to meet the demands of feeding people now and later. Growing food became a big business.

3

The Business of Growing Food

Today farming is big business. Most farms are owned by families or family partnerships. These are several families working together as a company. About 3 percent of farms are industrial farms or operations. These are large-scale farms.[1] Aiming to make more money, many farms today specialize. They grow only one type of crop. Or they grow only those crops that are in great demand. Ranches, which raise animals for meat, also focus on one type of meat, such as beef.

In the past, farms were run differently than they are today. A traditional farm included animals, or livestock. These were raised for meat, milk, or eggs. The fields included many different crops. Some were planted in different seasons or to help restore the soil. The parts of the farm interconnected. Manure from the cows was spread over the fields and plowed with the soil. This added nitrogen to the soil before planting. Animals ate corn or grain grown on the farm, along with straw. Straw is leftover from the wheat harvest.

When traditional farmers picked their crops, they sent most to buyers. Buyers would then send the produce or grain to locations where different stores and markets purchased it. A small part of the harvest was kept for the workers on the farm. And some of it was sold at roadside stands and farmers' markets.

Farmers' markets were a traditional way of selling produce. As supermarkets became more common in the

Dairy cows feed from their individual stalls. Most farms focus on one crop or one type of animal, such as dairy or beef cattle.

1950s, this tradition lapsed. Farmers began selling to large companies. These companies shipped the food all over the country and the world. According to organic farmer Jim Goodman, nonfarm families even stopped planting backyard gardens.[2] It was much easier to get everything they needed at the grocery store.

Industrial Farms

Around this time farming became industrialized. Big farms have become the norm, says Dr. James Horne, former director of Ag, the agricultural division of the Environmental Protection Agency (EPA). Big farms need big equipment and high-horsepower tractors. "As they roll across the fields, their weight compacts the soil, taking out airspaces," Horne explains. This prevents the soil from holding water. So the water runs off and the soil erodes. Compacting the soil also hurts the plant roots.[3]

Machines and large farm equipment replaced the work of farmworkers, called farmhands. Bigger equipment allowed farmers to plant more land, yielding a larger harvest. Bigger harvests meant they could make more money. It also meant the farmers needed different methods of planting. For example, they used fertilizer instead of manure.

These new methods fit the size and style of the bigger equipment. However, the fertilizer was more expensive. So was the bigger equipment. Now the farmer had to plant more land to get a larger crop to cover these new expenses. And larger fields meant more fertilizer and pest control. It went on and on.

As the population grew, more food was needed. This put a lot of pressure on farmers. It did not matter if the farm was small or a large company farm. The expectations for yield—how large the harvest is for a single type of crop—kept increasing. The focus became raising or growing whatever food was in demand.

Growing and Raising Food Today

Most industrial farms specialize. They either grow crops or raise animals. Crops come from plants. Crop farms grow vegetables, grains, or fruit. Potatoes, tomatoes, salad greens, cucumbers, carrots, and citrus are in demand. At the grocery store you will see plenty of these vegetables. Other major crops in the United States today are corn, soybeans, hay, wheat, cotton, rice, and a grain called sorghum used in animal feed.[4]

Several steps lead to a harvest. The farmer needs to get the soil ready. The soil is tilled, or the top layer turned under. Residue from the last crop is tilled under. The standard way is using a moldboard plow. But that left no residue on top. Today conservation tilling leaves up to 30 percent residue. This residue is good. It helps keep the topsoil from blowing or washing away.

A herbicide is sprayed to keep weeds from growing. Grain drills and planters allow many seeds to be planted as the tractor passes over the soil. After the crop begins to grow, nutrients are sprayed on plants. Nitrogen, phosphorous, and potassium are used along with fertilizer or manure. The crops are watered and sprayed with pesticides. These chemicals keep mice and insects away. Some kill fungus and weeds. Finally the crop is harvested.

Most food travels long distances to reach markets. The average distance is about 1,500 miles.[5] To prevent rotting during shipping, many fruits and vegetables are picked before they are ripe. Some ripen during transport. This happens naturally. All plants have ethylene, a plant hormone. It is important for plants to grow, mature, ripen, and age. It is naturally made by most fruits and vegetables. Apples, pears, peaches, melons, bananas, tomatoes, and avocados make large amounts of it. Ethylene can be used to ripen these fruits and vegetables if they are picked before they are ripe. This is called gassing. Fruits and vegetables are placed in a ripening room. Ethylene is piped in. It triggers ripening. More is naturally produced as the food ripens. Some vegetables, such as broccoli, cabbage, cauliflower, and lettuce, make only small amount of ethylene. They are highly sensitive to it. Too much exposure can shorten the shelf life of these foods.[6]

Farmers' markets sell food that is grown locally. This helps nearby farmers, and it reduces the distance that the food has to travel to reach your table.

Choosing Natural or Organic Foods

As shoppers become aware of what goes into food, more want healthier choices. But those choices can feel overwhelming. Is natural better than organic? It is a personal choice. No chemicals are used to grow organic foods. No preservatives are added to packaged food. Organic foods will have labels marking them as chemical free. Natural foods use no chemicals or preservatives in packaging. The following will help you sort out food labels to make healthy food choices.

USDA Organic	100% or 95% free of chemicals, pesticides, antibiotics, hormones, and synthetic additives. Made with organic ingredients that contain at least 70% organically grown food.
Natural/All Natural	contain no preservatives, chemicals, or additives; ingredients may not be organically grown.
Bird Friendly or Shade Grown	on coffee and tea products. Plants grown under trees that provide shade and a habitat for migratory birds.
Cage-free/ Free Range	eggs or poultry products. Birds are not kept in cages and animals have access to open air.
Grass-fed/Open Pasture	ideally, animals forage for food outdoors in a pasture; can also mean they are fed grass while in a pen
Pasture raised	animals roam freely outdoors and eat grass and plants.

Fair Trade Certified	on coffee, tea, chocolate, rice, or sugar means farmers received a fair price for their products and farmworkers were treated and paid fair wages.
Marine Stewardship Council	on frozen fish or Alaskan salmon means the seafood was caught without harming the ocean ecosystem and without endangering other species.
American Humane Certified	for bison, chicken, cows, pigs, sheep, and turkeys certifies the humane treatment of farm animals—they are not raised in cages, are allowed to engage in normal behaviors, and are tended by trained handlers.
Certified Humane Raised and Handled	for chickens, cows, pigs, and sheep—ensures animals are allowed enough space to move naturally, not kept in cages, treated humanely (no debeaking of poultry) and feed is free of hormones and antibiotics.
Animal Welfare Approved	for chickens, cows, ducks, geese, pigs, rabbits, sheep, and turkeys—bans the use of ties, tethers, crates, and cages and ensures access to pastures. Also protects animals from breeding for fast growth and from the fumes of their own waste.[7]

Meat Production

Farmers who raise animals for meat are called producers. They might raise cows or cattle to produce beef. They might raise pigs or hogs to produce pork. Poultry producers raise chickens, ducks, or turkeys. Dairy farms raise milk cows. Dairy farms produce milk. The milk from the cows is sold to dairy companies.

Some cattle ranches and dairy farms have pasture land. The animals roam and graze. The animals forage or look for food. The farmers supplement the forage with feed. Dairy farms that use this method focus on quality of milk instead of amount of the milk. For milk producers, the higher the fat, protein, and buttermilk the better. These are used to make cheese, yogurt, and other dairy products. A stall method is used for most milk cows. This means many cows are housed in one building. Each cow has a separate narrow stall with access to the feeding trough. The milking parlor is a similar row of narrow stalls. The cows are milked using a machine that collects and stores the milk in large tanks.

Most meat producers keep the animals together in large buildings. The temperature and lighting are controlled. Slotted floors are raised above a concrete base. This is more comfortable than standing or lying on concrete.

The fate of each animal is decided at birth. Most will become food. Some will go to a breeder house. They give birth to more animals. Cattle and pigs follow similar stages. The animal is born. When it is old enough to be taken from the mother it goes to the nursery building. This is called the feedlot for beef cows and cattle. The animals grow until they reach a specific size. Then they go to a finishing building. Here they are fed or fattened until they reach market size. For pigs this is 240 to 275 pounds and takes five to six months.[8]

Poultry Production

Eggs, chicken, and turkey meat are a healthy part of many diets today. In the early 1900s, chicken was eaten only on Sundays. Turkey was eaten on Thanksgiving and Christmas. It is now an everyday food.

Farmers in the United States raise over 43 billion pounds of poultry meat annually. According to the USDA Economic Research Service, about one fifth is turkey and the rest is chicken. The United States is the top producer and exporter of poultry in the world, and the second largest for eggs.[9] Chickens are raised mainly in the southern and southeastern United States. Turkeys are raised in northern states. Egg production is spread across the country.

The birds are kept inside large buildings. This protects them from weather and wild animals, which

Chickens on a poultry farm. U.S. farmers raise more
than 43 billion pounds of poultry meat every year.

might attack the hens or spread disease. As with beef and pork production, the fate of the birds is decided when they hatch. Chickens are raised for three different functions. Each is housed on different parts of a poultry farm. Most chicks become part of the broiler flock. Broilers, or chickens under thirteen weeks old, are raised for meat. According to the U.S. Broiler Industry, 8.6 million broilers were raised on U.S. farms in 2009.[10] Some hens will become part of the laying flock or the breeding flock. The laying flock produces eggs for market. The breeding flock lays eggs sent to the hatchery. These produce more birds for meat.

Lighting is very important for the growth of chickens, ducks, and turkeys. These birds are kept in blackout houses. Artificial lighting is used to control their growth. Ducks are the fastest growing of poultry birds. They will reach seven pounds in six or seven weeks. Turkeys take longest. They are ready for market in fifteen to twenty-five weeks. That is about six months.[11]

A Return to Natural Farming

Many animals are kept in these buildings. Farmers keep them healthy with antibiotics. Sometimes the animals are given shots or vaccines. Sometimes antibiotics are added to the feed. Some farmers give the animals hormones so they will produce more meat. This is similar to using chemicals in growing crops. The fertilizer feeds the soil. Herbicide kills weeds so plants can thrive. But do the chemicals get into the food? Does the meat contain antibiotics and hormones?

Many people think so. As early as the 1940s, people realized heavy use of fertilizer would damage the soil. According to agriculturist Dr. James E. Horne, one of these believers was J. I. Rodale. Rodale founded Rodale Press, publisher of *Organic Gardening* and *Prevention* magazines. He also wrote books on organic farming in the 1940s and 1950s.[12]

Organic farming returned to the old ways of growing crops. Instead of using fertilizer, manure is used. Sometimes crops are grown simply to turn under and enrich the soil. This is called green manure and was used in Abraham Lincoln's time, explains Horne. Insects that eat other insects are used for pest control, he says.[13] Both limit chemicals.

Soil is tilled to prevent loss of topsoil. Crops are rotated in the fields. Each new crop adds to the soil. Each year the soil becomes richer. Chemicals left from industrial farming are slowly stripped away. Organic farmers also conserve water and energy. There are strict guidelines to follow if a farmer wants to be certified as an organic farmer.

According to environmental writer Bryan A. McCarty, "The fields must be free from [chemicals, pesticides and man-made fertilizers] for at least three years before the farmer can harvest an organic crop. Once the three years has passed, the farmer must pay for the government-approved inspector to examine the land and declare its certification as an organic farm."[14]

These costs are passed along, states Lisa Roberts, reporter for the *Orlando Sentinel*. "The farms are also smaller. Often the harvests are smaller."[15]

Still, more parents are buying organic food "to keep their children's diets free of food grown with pesticides, hormones, antibiotics or genetic engineering," states journalist Libby Quaid.[16] The toxins in foods are more dangerous for children. Children need to eat more for their size than adults. This is because their bodies are growing very fast. So are their brains. Because they eat more food, they end up with more of the chemicals used to grow or raise that food, she explained.

Roberts explains that some foods have more left-over pesticide even after washing. These are called the "dirty dozen." Many people will choose organic when they buy these foods. The dirty dozen are: apples, bell peppers, celery, cherries, imported grapes, nectarines, peaches, pears, potatoes, red raspberries, spinach, and strawberries. Other fruits and vegetables have low pesticide levels, says Roberts. Those include asparagus, avocados, bananas, broccoli, cauliflower, sweet corn, kiwi, mangoes, onions, papaya, pineapples, and sweet peas.[17]

It is not just what you eat. According to food writer Christie Matheson, "All those pesticides and chemical fertilizers are used to produce our juice, milk, coffee, tea, wine, and cocktails, too." Rain forests are clear-cut in order to grow coffee. This allows the sun to reach the plants. Then they will grow faster. But destroying rain forests forces birds into extinction and increases greenhouse gases in the air. "Luckily, organic and shade-grown coffee is easy to find, as are organic cocoa and wine," says Matheson.[18]

Many owners of small farms use organic farming methods. But, it is expensive to go through the steps to become certified as an organic grower. So, they grow without chemicals or pesticides. They sell to restaurants and markets just as other farmers do. Buying from these local farmers may have an added benefit. You are helping the local economy. But you will also be getting organic food without the added cost.

Michael Pollan, journalist and author of four food books, explains that we have shifted from the original plan for organic farming. "There were three legs to the original organic dream."[19] Food was supposed to grow in harmony with nature. This meant animals were treated well. They roamed in fresh air outdoors.

You Can: Buy Local

Buying food from local farmers has a bigger impact than you realize. It supports your community. Your dollars stay local. In a sense, you are investing in that farm. Farms, according to Pollan, "produce a kind of landscape."[20] The money you spend buying locally helps conserve that landscape.

Sometimes people in the community pledge to help cover the cost of running a local farm. This is called community-supported agriculture (CSA). Each member who pledges shares both the risks and benefits with the farmer. Throughout the year, members receive "shares" or some of the harvest from the farm.[21]

The food is fresher. This means your body gets to use more of the nutrients. It also saves fuel. The food is not shipped to food-packing plants and then to the grocery store. Pollan says, "When you buy local you're voting for a short, highly legible food chain—one that supports all three legs of the original vision. The shorter food chain brings consumer and producer together, and the producer gets to tell her story."[22] You get to know the farmer. You know where the food came from and how it was grown. Farmers' markets and local farms also sell eggs, milk, and hothouse greens in winter. "With every food purchasing decision, we are helping to create the world we want to live in, one bite at a time," says Pollan.[23]

Community newspapers often post notices for upcoming farmers' markets. They are held on the weekends. In some areas they are set up in a parking lot. You can also find farms in your area. Look in the phone book or enter your zip code on the Local Harvest Web site.

They ate feed but also grazed for food. No chemicals were used on plants.

The second leg was how the food came to the table. Organic food was sold through farmers' markets. People bought from local farmers. And, the variety of the food was large. This was the third leg. People had choice in many different kinds of apples, for instance.[24]

Pollan says that once standards were set up for organic farmers they began to lose control of their purpose in farming naturally. The standards were thought to be necessary, he explains. In order to sell their food to big companies and get it into conventional supermarkets, some guidelines were needed. "Today the organic dream is in peril. In fact, many of the best farmers in this country no longer even use the word *organic*."[25] Today, he says, we have "organic food forced through the industrial system, shorn of its holism. What has been lost is that key insight about organic: that everything is connected. The organic dream has been reduced to a farming method."[26]

So how did it come to this? To understand, we need to return to a time just after World War II. The goal at that time was to stop world hunger. Somehow, farmers needed to find a way to produce more food and get it to the people of the world. The efforts to do this became known as the "Green Revolution."

4

The Green Revolution

Farmers began feeling the pressure for larger harvests during World War I. Wheat was shipped to Europe and other countries. After the war, more people left the country to live in the city. The Roaring Twenties was going strong. People in the cities, who could not grow their own food, depended on the harvests of farmers.

One of the first hybrid crops was grown in the 1920s. It crossed two types of corn for a hardier stalk. This hybrid resisted a corn blight that had wiped out corn crops in the past.[1] People were suspicious of the "man-made" corn, but in time it caught on and became readily available.

During World War II, farmers again planted to meet demands. They had to feed the troops and people overseas. Farmers worked to meet the demand for wheat, corn, fruit, and vegetables needed to feed the country.

Agriculturalists, or scientists who study plants and the best ways to grow them, came up with ideas for better ways to plant crops.

Like the corn blight, wheat crops were often ruined by disease. During the 1950s, wheat rust, a type of fungus, attacked crop fields in the Midwest. A stronger wheat was needed, one that would stand up to disease.

Green Revolution

Dr. Norman Borlaug was the leading scientist in this effort. He began his work with wheat in the early 1950s. "A new race of rust destroyed more than 300 million

Wheat rust is a disease that can destroy a harvest.

bushels of wheat in 1954 alone," according to Leon Hesser, an agricultural economist.[2] What made this even more of a problem was wind. Wind carried the rust spores to the southern United States and Mexico. In the spring, winds carried the rust spores from Mexico north into the United States.

This type of problem is solved by crossbreeding two different types of wheat. Normally, the new variety is planted. At harvest, seeds from the best plants are used to crossbreed. "Borlaug crossed hundreds and hundreds because he couldn't wait the 6–7 years the usual process took. He had to speed the process," explained Hesser.[3]

Borlaug worked on the new wheat in Mexico. The farmers he worked with had farms in two different regions. In one area wheat grew in the summer. In the other, it grew in the winter. To speed the process he convinced the farmers to try the new wheat in both places. Seeds were shuttled between the two locations. One was in a high altitude. The other was at sea level. The wheat grew in both places. From those harvests Borlaug selected the best seeds. He continued crossbreeding.

This shuttle-breeding program cut the time needed to get results in half, stated Hesser.[4] Borlaug was able to grow two generations per year. The wheat was "exposed to different diseases, different soils, different climates and different day lengths," Hesser explained.[5]

They also grew at two different altitudes. This new wheat was not only rust resistant but highly adaptable. It grew in a range of conditions. So it would grow throughout the world.

Another result of Borlaug's work was a shorter wheat plant. Taller plants fell over when fertilizer was applied. These shorter plants did not. "Yields skyrocketed," says Hesser.[6] This meant that each crop produced much more wheat. By 1956, Borlaug had developed forty new varieties of wheat. The yield nearly doubled. This made Mexico self-sufficient in wheat production.

Borlaug also found innovative ways to crossbreed plants. In 1970, he received the Nobel Peace Prize for this work. What made his work even more remarkable is that the achievement was made in a short time. "Advances in agriculture typically are gradual," explains Hesser.[7]

Feeding the World

Many countries depended on the United States to supply their corn, wheat, and other crops. During the 1960s, the goal became finding a way to help these countries feed their own people.

Farmers and scientists worked together to stop world hunger. Borlaug's work triggered a worldwide effort to increase food production in developing countries. Some scientists worked with rice and others with maize, or

Norman Borlaug (second from left) worked to create a new breed of wheat that would be resistant to stem rust.

corn. They modeled Borlaug's work with wheat. They also did crossbreeding to create stronger plants. These stronger, healthier plants were high-yield varieties. This meant they produced a larger harvest. These high-yield varieties of corn, rice, and wheat were introduced in countries such as Mexico and India.

Borlaug's research took place in Mexico. The subtropic weather made many crops difficult to grow. People in this area were hungry. So there was a need for high yields at harvest. These conditions helped create a type of wheat that could be grown in many places.

His research produced new knowledge. His efforts brought new technology to these farmers. They could use it on small tracts of land as well as on large farms.

You Can: Help Prevent World Hunger

You may not be a scientist, but there is something you can do to help feed the world. Heifer International is a group that strives to end world hunger. They do this by providing sustainable food sources. For example, a cow provides milk. The milk can be sold. This provides some income. Seeds can be planted. The plants provide food. The food can be sold to provide income. Seeds are collected to continue planting and benefitting from the gift of seeds. The farmers learn how to feed themselves now and also in the future. These gifts are made to families or villages.

They do not only receive the gifts. Volunteers teach them about the environment. They are taught how to keep their plot of land or animal healthy. They learn how to care for the earth. Those who receive gifts must agree to "pass on the gift." This means they give offspring of their gift to another family.[8]

Pitch in with friends or family to raise money to donate an animal through Heifer International. Visit their Web site to learn about sustainable living and for ideas on how you can raise money to give a gift.

The methods to create these stronger varieties used newly bred plant varieties. These newer plants needed a lot of fertilizer. According to agricultural economist Terry L. Anderson, the use of chemical fertilizers by American farmers more than quadrupled.[9] But these new plant varieties used both water and fertilizer very well. They also grew in a range of conditions. This meant the farmer was less likely to lose a crop to disease, overly rainy seasons, or overly dry seasons.

In developing countries, farmers were taught different ways of farming, which mimicked industrial farming in developed nations. They used fertilizer and pesticides.

"In the past forty years, hybrid grains have made modern agriculture spectacularly productive," says Horne. He points out that corn plants are uniform in height. They also form ears at the same time. Like the crops the scientists created using crossbreeding, these plants all have high yields. Horne explains: "They have been bred to respond to chemical fertilizers and have uniform growth habits adapted to farm machinery."[10]

The "Green Revolution" did succeed in increasing food harvests. But, according to organic farmer Jim Goodman, it did little for food quality. "Industrial production of the cheap food that fills our supermarkets is slowly starving us."[11] By cheap food, Goodman

Did Bioengineering Go Astray?

Dr. Borlaug's shuttle-breeding method sped up the process for combining two species of plants. Scientists looked for other ways to speed up the process for creating hardier plants or animals. The result was bioengineered foods. Bioengineering modifies the genes of one species with another. For example, the genes from a wild potato that resists potato blight is placed into a potato variety grown for food. These foods are called genetically modified, or GM foods. GM is often compared to extremely rapid selective breeding. The best traits from the hardiest plants or the healthiest animals are combined to help farmers produce more food quickly.

Genes from animals or micro-organisms can be inserted into plants. This is one way plants were modified to repel certain insects and reduce the need for pesticides. Commonly grown foods, such as many varieties of squash, corn, potatoes, soybeans, and tomatoes, have been genetically modified. The FDA regulates GM foods, including genetically engineered (GE) animals. According to the FDA, "Although conventional breeding methods have been used for a long time to select for desirable traits in animals, genetic engineering is a much more targeted and powerful method of actually introducing specific desirable traits into animals."[12]

The goal of GM or GE foods is increasing the supply of food through higher yield or quicker maturity, better tasting and more nutritious food that uses fewer chemicals, and eliminating disease. For example, some milk cows are susceptible to a disease of the udder. GE results in cows that do not suffer from this blight. This creates healthier cows and higher milk production.

Still there are those opposed to GM and GE foods. Opponents feel the risks are high. The biggest concern is that unexpected or harmful results could take place if modified specifies cross with natural specifies of plants or animals. According to a Healthline report, "Some people have raised concerns that the genes from one food that are inserted into another food may cause an allergic reaction. For instance, if peanut genes are in tomatoes, could someone with a peanut allergy react to tomatoes?"[13]

The FDA reviews scientific and safety information before deeming GM and GE foods safe for production and consumer use.

and other organic farmers mean that mass-production of food depletes the soil, which in turn affects the quality of the food grown in that soil. The Green Revolution tried to help farmers grow food more efficiently. It was driven by the need to protect plants and animals from disease. This led to more bountiful harvests. But as farmers worked to grow more and more food in order to feed more and more people, they resorted to methods that organic farmers believe are hurtful in the long run. Mass-production of food, in the eyes of organic farmers such as Goodman, meant a decline in food quality and a rise in scares over food safety. Both reflect poorly on food production and marketing. These failures will drive food production back to the local level. Local farmers know that healthy food comes only from healthy soil. Making the soil healthy again will produce quality food high in nutrition. "Local producers worldwide know that hands-on farming affords a better way to care for the soil and produce healthy food," Goodman says.[14]

5

Food Security

Plants need nutrients to grow, just as people do. Like people, plants use nutrients for energy and to build and maintain cells. Sunlight, air, water, and soil are all vital for plants to survive. A plant takes root in the soil. The roots take water and nutrients from the soil.

As the plant sprouts from the seed, it uses the seed pod as food. As roots take hold in the soil, the plant begins to draw on the soil for what it needs. The roots draw minerals and other nutrients from the soil into the plant. The plant uses energy from the sun. The leaves convert, or change, sunlight and carbon dioxide from the air into chlorophyll. The plant thrives. Remove any one of these elements and the plant dies.

Conventional farming uses a lot of chemicals. Pesticides and fertilizers are meant to help the plants grow and produce bountiful harvests. But whatever does not get on the plants goes into the soil. Later, after harvest, the plant dies and is plowed into the soil. The chemicals absorbed into the plant are now added to the soil. When this happens year after year, the chemicals in the soil may build and prevent the new plants from getting the nutrients they need out of the soil. This heavy use of chemicals in farming today creates risk to future food harvests.

Harvest at Risk

Each type of plant needs different nutrients. Unless the nutrients taken from the soil by a plant are returned, the soil eventually wears out. It is no longer fertile. Agriculturist Jim Horne compares soil to a rubber band. "A rubber band is resilient but not infinitely so. Pull on it hard for too long and it loses its elasticity."[1] This is what too much chemical use has done to soil, he says. Farmers need to get all they can out of the land they farm. So they are forced to use methods that "may cause erosion or jeopardize the life and health of the soil in some other way."[2]

After the crop is harvested, the rest of the plant dies. It is plowed under, adding nutrients to the soil. But it cannot add the nutrients used by the grain or vegetable that has been harvested. It can only add what is left after the harvest. Traditional farming rotated crops.

Wheat harvest in Akron, Ohio. After a crop is harvested, what is left of the plant is plowed under, adding nutrients to the soil.

Something different was grown in the plot, so the dead plant added new nutrients to the soil after harvest. When the same crops are grown in the same plot of soil year after year, the soil becomes worn out. This is called monoculture. Unless the depleted nutrients are added to the soil, the plant will have fewer and fewer minerals to allow it to thrive. The grain, fruit, or vegetable may still grow, but may not be as big. It may not taste quite as good. The yield, or amount, of each plant may be lower than the year before.

Jim Horne compares industrial farms to machines in a factory. "The machinery is ready, the routine is known, and the markets are there. But the soil is not a machine that produces crops. It is organic—alive, not dead. Monoculture depletes the soil of its life and health."[3]

Traditional farming rotated crops grown in each field. During winter, some fields might grow a winter crop, such as winter wheat. In other fields, a cover crop is grown. A cover crop is not a cash crop. It does not get harvested to add to income. A cover crop keeps the nutrient-rich topsoil from blowing away. In the spring, it gets plowed under. These plants added nutrients to the soil.

Conventional farming added fertilizer or chemicals to the soil to boost nutrients. "Fertilizers, it was thought, could make up for loss of fertile topsoil. The long-term effects of such farming practices have not been given enough weight or have been ignored in favor of short-term gain," acording to Horne.[4] Huge equipment was used to plow and chop the top soil. It turned the soil under, spread fertilizer, and sprayed pesticides. The goal of conventional farming is to grow more for higher yield. This is done by planting and harvesting faster. The more a farmer grows, the greater his profit. People all over the world depend on the farmer's good harvest. Even with all this equipment and chemical help, a lot can go wrong—too much rain, too little rain, or disease that kills or damages plants.

Erosion

Pressure to produce more and more food causes farmers to plow land they have not farmed in the past. Trees planted along a field are removed so that tract of land can be plowed. "Too often the shelter belts of trees, the sod waterways, the terraces, and other conservation measures proven to increase moisture and stop erosion in fields are abandoned or destroyed when a farmer deems they are cutting into his profits," says Horne.[5]

These trees are important, though. They keep the wind from drying out the ground and eroding the fields. They provide shelter to insects, birds, and animals. Many of these creatures benefit the farmer, too. They eat pests that would ruin the crop.

Where trees once stood, crops now grow in rows. "Unfortunately, this practice has been heavily supported by government programs that were designed to reduce a farmer's financial risk."[6]

A return to traditional farming helps counter this problem. Traditional farmers use methods that maintain the land. They rebuild the land. Instead of stripping trees in order to plant more crops, trees are planted in rows along the edge of the fields. These are called shelterbelts. They block the wind. This keeps topsoil from blowing away. This is especially important when the field is empty. Winter winds can stir up and blow away topsoil.

Farmers reduce their financial risk by sending food all over the world. Globalization of food has advantages. During winter months, we get fruit and vegetables from warmer climates. Fruits such as kiwi, acai, and pomegranate are available from other countries. The same is true with vegetables. But, says Goodman, globalization has disadvantages, too. The food that ends up at the supermarkets "is mass-produced by underpaid farmers and farm workers," he says.[7]

Healing the Soil

Soil that is worn out can be restored. A Cuban-born soil scientist, Pedro Sanchez, proved it. He won the World Food Prize in 2002. It honors work he did to replenish poor soil in Africa. According to journalist Elizabeth Weise, in 2002, in sub-Saharan Africa, about 180 million people did "not know where their next meal [was] coming from."[8] The soil in Africa is shallow. During many years of farming, it had lost its nutrients. Nitrogen was especially lacking. Conventional farming adds nitrogen using fertilizer. This method is very expensive in Africa. It cost 200 to 600 percent more to buy fertilizer than anywhere else in the world. Another way was desperately needed.

Sanchez and his colleagues came up with a plan that took conditions in Africa into account. "At the beginning of rainy season, farmers interplant corn—a dietary staple—with local varieties of fast-growing trees that can take nitrogen from the air by using bacteria in their roots," explains Weise.[9]

At first, the trees grow very slowly. Around the time the corn is ready for harvest, the trees hit a growth spurt. They can grow up to nine feet in eight months. They are allowed to grow for the crop season. This takes a full year. "Just before the next planting cycle, when the rains are ready to begin, the farmers cut down the trees. The leaves are dug into the soil. Doing this can add 247 to 494 pounds of vital nitrogen to each acre of soil," says Weise.[10] The wood from the trees is used for firewood. Wood from four-fifths of an acre is enough for one family for one year, she explains. This protects against deforestation.

But there are two more parts to Sanchez's plan. In addition to nitrogen, African soil needs phosphorous. Africa has many deposits of rock phosphates. These are rocks that contain the mineral phosphorous. Fertilizer companies have ignored these deposits because they are too small to collect profitably. But small farmers can collect these rocks, crush them, and add them to the soil. The acidity naturally in the soil helps break down the rock. This creates a form of phosphorous the soil can use. Next, farmers gather a weedy shrub called Mexican sunflower, whose leaves contain many nutrients. It grows along roadsides and along farm boundaries from Ethiopia to South Africa. Farmers chop the stems and leaves into small pieces. They place them at the bottom of planting holes along with the seed. "This provides micronutrients for healthy growth," states Weise.[11]

When such simple methods are matched to the conditions of the farm environment, crop yield can double or quadruple. It also gives farmers a chance to grow other types of crops.

Water Quality

Plants need rich soil, sun, and water to grow. Droughts are periods of little rain. This dry weather hurts plants.

Taste the "Place" of Your Food

Terroir (pronounced tehr-WAHR) is a French word that means "land" or "soil." The idea behind terroir farming is that foods grown in different places have distinct flavors. Plants absorb nutrients from the soil, so they can take on the characteristics or flavors of the land. "Terroir is the voice of the land as sung through agriculture," says award-winning food writer Dara Moskowitz.[12]

Originally, the term was used for wines. The grapes used in making wine grow in different climates. So winemakers matched the grape vine to different growing locations. Over time, the wines made with these grapes reflected the land on which they were grown. Grapes grown in California sun, with a breeze off the ocean and quick-draining volcanic soil, might end up with a bright, concentrated flavor. Those grown at the edge of the sea might taste rich with a hint of sea mist from the water's minerals.

The same concept is used among some organic farmers who grow their product so it will express the taste of the land. Moskowitz explains that such growers have a reverence for the land and wish to voice it through the flavor of their products. They carefully select and plant so the harvest produces a product "that communicates the soul of the land as we have come to understand it."[13] She uses artichokes as an example. They grow best near the sea where the air is not too hot nor too cold. Whether grown in Southern California or various places in Italy, the artichoke will have flavors of its microclimate along with the "nutty, woody, grassy, meaty divinity of the artichoke," she says.[14] In comparison, those grown by scientists who have bred them in greenhouses and in deserts, she says, taste of "watery cardboard."[15]

If it does not rain often enough, farmers must water their crops. This is called irrigation. Often, water use is limited or the cost of water goes up during times of drought. So farmers cannot afford to water as much. These water shortages add to the problem. Plants that do not get enough water and are not growing in rich soil will not grow well. They may be smaller than normal, or they may not yield much at harvest.

"It is basic," says Horne. "Sun, soil, and water make life possible. Although good rich soil is becoming more difficult to find in the fields of America, water, too, is another natural resource equally at risk."[16]

David Mackay writes about agriculture and the environment. He describes water as "this liquid of life."[17] He explains that a rise in the cost of water will make food prices go up. The added cost is passed on to those buying the food. Also, water shortages can limit the amount of food the farmer is able to grow. "Scientific studies show that drought is occurring for longer periods and more often," he says.[18]

This is happening around the world. In the southern and western United States, Australia, and Europe, drought is devastating wheat and grain crops. Scientists are working to develop drought-resistant varieties. These would grow well with very little water.

Humans who eat foods made from grain, such as bread, pasta, and cereal, are not the only ones to suffer.

An agronomist and farmers discuss the drought that caused this irrigation ditch near Rio Bravo, Mexico, to dry up.

Some of the grain crop is used in animal feed. According to Mackay, drought has affected dairy production, especially in Australia.[19]

It does not end with the farmers and the food they grow. Water is needed for food packaging. If the water supply is limited, the company has two options. They can process less food. Or they can pass the rising cost of water to those who buy the food.

Organic farmers run into these problems, too. Though their soil is healthy, crops still need water.

You Can: Choose (Almost) All Veggies

Many people choose to cut back on the amount of meat they eat. Others decide to eat no meat. They are called vegetarians. Vegetarians eat mostly fruits, vegetables, beans, and grains. They do not eat meat, fish, or fowl (such as chicken or turkey). There are several types of vegetarian diets. Lacto vegetarians eat no meat, fish, fowl, or eggs. They do eat dairy products. Ovo vegetarian eat no meat, fish, fowl, or dairy products. They do eat eggs. Lacto-ovo vegetarians eat no meat, fish, or fowl. But they eat both eggs and dairy products.[20] Eating better is the goal. A vegetarian diet offers many health benefits—for example, lower cholesterol and fat content and higher fiber and vitamins.

According to Vegan Outreach, "Simply avoiding animal products, however, will not ensure optimal health. Like  everyone, vegans should eat a well-balanced diet. Protein, vitamins B12 and D, omega-3 fats, calcium, and iodine are important."[21]

A pure vegetarian diet is called vegan. Vegans eat only plant-based food. They do not eat any products coming from animals. This means they do not eat eggs, dairy products, or even honey. They get their protein from soy and plant protein. Rice, soy, nut, and seed products provide dairy alternatives.

An important factor in a vegetarian diet is the variety of foods eaten. A vegetarian diet is not a good choice for

a picky eater. According to dietitian Reed Mangels, PhD, "The teens years are times of especially rapid growth and change with high nutritional needs."[22] Protein, essential amino acids, iron, calcium, and vitamins D and B12 are generally provided through meat, eggs, and dairy products. Depending on the type of vegetarian diet a person follows, she would eat a variety of foods to meet the recommended daily allowance (RDA). For example, brown rice, whole grain bread, oatmeal, tofu, green leafy vegetables such as spinach and kale, broccoli, black-eyed peas, chickpeas, and beans are good choices.

The Vegetarian Resource Group is a good place for parents and teens to find answers to questions about vegetarian diets and nutrition. Protein is among the first concern parents have when teens consider becoming vegetarian. An adult male would receive the RDA for protein by eating 1 cup of oatmeal, 1 cup of soy milk, 2 slices of whole wheat bread, 1 bagel, 2 tablespoons of peanut butter, 1 cup of vegetarian baked beans, 5 ounces of tofu, 2 tablespoons of almonds, 1 cup of broccoli, and 1 cup of brown rice.[23] Before making the switch to a vegetarian diet, it is important to consult your doctor or see a nutritionist. Choosing to simply cut back on meat is also a valid choice. It is important to make sure you get all the nutrition you need from your diet—whatever you choose to eat.

During a drought, plants create less food to harvest. The food-packaging plants that make organic products also use water to process the food. A shortage means higher food prices.

Lost Genetic Diversity

The quality of the soil and the quality of the water affect how well a plant grows. But what about the plant itself? One amazing result of the Green Revolution was plants bred from only the hardiest plants. As one type of grain or tomato was crossed with another, those original varieties were lost. About 75 percent of the diversity of crops has been lost, according to the United Nations Food and Agricultural Organization.[24]

Horne argues that having many types of the same plant is important. This diversity ensures that increasing numbers of people can be fed. The variety of plant genes provide "insurance for the future—against changes in climate, such as possible global warming, evolving pests and diseases, and changes in the availability of energy, along with changes in fashion, markets, and the structure of agriculture."[25]

The problem also occurs among animals raised for meat. The farms operate in selecting the best of the animals to use for breeding. According to Horne, they are selected to produce "a standard carcass profile, rapid weight gain, and ability to utilize high-concentrate feed."[26] This ensures that the animals grow big and are ready for market quickly. Uniform size and shapes make the processing of the meat faster. This aids the meat-packing companies.

Any animals that do not fit this profile are not used for breeding, so their genes die out. According to the American Livestock Breeds Conservancy, about eighty breeds of cattle and pigs and many varieties of poultry are in danger of extinction.[27] The gene pool for live-stock is becoming limited. Horne explains what this means. Traits that do not matter in rapid production of animals for meat are important for other types of farms. For instance, such traits might include adaptability to different types of climate or a strong instinct to protect and care for their young. If animals with these traits are not bred, they become extinct.[28]

Organic farmers may not continue this selective process. But some of the species of both crops and animals are already lost. The standards for organic farming succeeded in removing chemicals and pesti-cides from the food we eat. But the guidelines only dealt with the manner in which food was grown or raised.

According to Michael Pollan, organic guidelines overlook other details. These are important, too. They relate to producing food in a way that is friendly to the environment. "There's nothing about the kind of food that may be called organic, or about distribution. There's

How Much Protein Do You Really Need?

The amount of protein you need depends on age, gender, and body size. It also changes based on how active you are. Adults need about 0.8 grams per kilogram of body weight. But children and teens need about 1.2 grams per kilogram. Finding out how much protein you need is simple.

Divide your body weight by 2.2. This gives you your weight in kilograms. Now, multiply that number by 1.2. This is how many grams of protein you need each day.[29]

Suppose you weigh 100 pounds: 100/2.2 = 45 kg
45 x 1.2 = 54 g
You would need 54 grams of protein per day.

no rule against high-fructose corn syrup. Myriad synthetics are allowed in processed organic food," Pollan says. "And we find ourselves with an organic trans-continental strawberry: 5 calories of food energy that require 435 calories of fossil-fuel to get to a supermarket near you."[30] The principles of organic farming have changed, but they need to go further. Sustainable farming is the key. We need to grow food that is healthy for people. We need to grow it in ways that are better for the earth. We need to make sure that the earth can sustain, or continue to provide, the amount of food that the world needs. This is why a New Green Revolution is needed.

6

The New Green Revolution

The New Green Revolution focuses on both the present and the future. Farmers work to produce enough food for today. But they also make sure the land will be able to grow or raise food in the future. The New Green Revolution is called sustainable farming. This type of farming tries to take the best of organic and industrial farming. But the methods are different. The goal is to produce the large amounts of food needed to feed the world. And wise use of machinery can make that job easier.

"Around the world, farmers and ranchers are experimenting with a different form of agriculture, a more sustainable way of producing and distributing food and fiber," states the Sustainable Agriculture and Research Education (SARE) program.[1] James Horne describes sustainable farming as a cross between ecology and agriculture. The way the farm is run must keep up with food needs. The farm must make money, but to continue doing so, it must stay healthy. Both the farmers and the farmworkers should be treated fairly and have a good quality of life, he says. "A sustainable agriculture will yield healthy rural communities and towns, which are key to the overall health of our nation."[2]

The condition of the soil is important. So is the goal of feeding people now and in the future. Sometimes crops are grown to replenish the soil when they are turned under. Crops are rotated each year. This means that tomato plants may be grown in one field this year, but next year the field will grow squash or beans or spinach. Chemical use is limited. If chemicals are needed to treat insects or rust, natural, plant-based ones are used. Synthetic (man-made) treatment is avoided.

Educating for Sustainable Farming

The need for more food means that farmers need to be more productive. Today each farmer feeds 129 people in the United States and abroad. In the 1930s, each farmer fed 9.8 people.[3] The question now is how to be more productive in a greener way. Sustainable farming is about using less fuel and fewer chemicals while producing as much food as possible.

Many cranberry growers have cut down on their use of pesticides and fertilizers.

In the United States, Congress passed a bill to help farmers with this job. They set up education programs to help farmers work toward sustainable farming. SARE encourages low-input farming. Many farmers thought this meant a return to the back-breaking labor of pre-World War II farming. That is not the case, explains Horne. Large farming equipment is still used, but its use is limited. Low-input means using fewer chemicals, which means using less fuel. When farmers are not spraying pesticides or spreading fertilizer as often, this means they are using less fuel because they are not running huge farm equipment as much as they used to. Many farmers are also finding alternative power and fuel sources, too.

The goal of SARE is to help farmers and ranchers increase profits. As farms prosper, so do farm families and communities. SARE also promotes environmental stewardship. They educate farmers on ways to improve soil and focus on renewable resources such as water and fertilizer. This relates to profits. Quality soil produces healthier plants. Healthier plants produce bigger harvests. Less chemical use creates healthier soil and plants. It also saves on the costs for running the farm.[4]

Farmers and ranchers have many options for sustainable production. According to SARE, ranchers can divide rangeland into sections. They rotate where the cattle graze, moving the herd from section to section. This allows one section to recover while another is being grazed. Natural resources, such as streams and soil, are better managed.

Crop farmers can cut costs and better manage resources in several ways. Farmland is also divided into sections. Different crops are planted each season. Cover crops are used to limit weed growth and replenish the soil. They also require fewer chemicals—pesticides, herbicides, and fertilizer—which save on costs.

Fruit and vegetable growers are encouraged to sell their harvest in different ways. They might sell directly to restaurants or schools. Farmers' markets, roadside stands, and Web sites are other options. These support the local community, especially when local residents are able to spend their food dollars at local markets and roadside stands.

Horne describes a wide variety of positive results from the SARE program. Use of herbicides, pesticides, and fertilizers was cut in half by cranberry growers in the Northeast. Farmers in Iowa devised a new way to till or plow the soil. It is called ridge tillage. It controls erosion. It also requires less fuel for plowing and fewer chemicals. In Florida, researchers found organic pest control options. They will reduce the exposure to pesticides many farmworkers have. They could also save growers about $400 per acre. Fruit and vegetable producers in Connecticut now supply Hartford schools

Traditional methods of plowing leave the soil unprotected, so that wind can blow dry soil away.

with fresh produce. This provides new markets but it has another bonus. Inner-city children get high-quality fresh food and also learn about nutrition and the environment. They participate in farm field days and cooking demonstrations by chefs.[5]

Smart Breeding

Another new approach to farming is smart breeding. It takes the idea of genetic modification (GM) to a new level. It could be called the new and improved GM crop, and so it is destined to put genetically modified crops out of business. Genetic modification develops new varieties by inserting genes from a desired animal or plant into an organism. Sometimes DNA from a plant is used to replace DNA in an animal cell. Sometimes animal DNA is added to plant DNA. For example, rather than having to spray pesticides to keep an insect from ruining a crop, GM can add an element from another plant or organism to keep the pests away. Antibiotics or vitamins can also be included through GM so that food is more nutritious. But combining the DNA of animals or organisms with plants raises fears for many people. The cause for alarm is unfounded, however. The FDA has found GM foods to be perfectly safe. In fact, most people have probably eaten GM foods many times without being aware of it. The FDA does not require

The Controversy Over Cloned Meat

Would you consider eating cloned meat? What about cloned vegetables? Would you know whether the food you ate was cloned? Probably not.

In January 2008, the FDA judged meat from cloned cows, pigs, and goats to be safe to eat, along with that of their offspring. For this reason, they decided there was no reason to label it.[6]

In science fiction stories and movies, clones are copies of the real person or animal. But a clone is not an exact copy. Health writer Andrew Lawler explains that DNA from a preferred animal is replaced with DNA in a host egg. This can be done with cells in plants or seeds. We have actually been eating vegetables and fruit for years that could be considered "clones."

Lawler says:

> Most of the bananas, potatoes, apples, and grapes at supermarkets are clones, having been produced through various "vegetative propaga-tion" techniques designed to ensure consistent quality and get produce to market quickly.[7]

In a 2006 survey by the Pew Initiative on Food and Biotechnology, more than 60 percent of those who responded did not like the idea of cloned meat; 40 percent said they would not serve it. People are worried about the safety of cloned meat and are also uncomfortable with the thought of it. "Skeptics are pushing lawmakers to force meat producers to label cloned meat and dairy products as such," states Lawler.[8]

The fact is, the cost of cloning is high. According to Lawler, it costs around $30,000 per animal. It also has high risks. Only 5 percent of cloned animals reach the stage of birth. Of those, few survive the first year of life, says Lawler.

At this point, he states, cloning is reserved for prize cattle and horses. Before we worry about whether we are eating cloned meat, consider the investment required for cloning. Breeders will likely keep those prize animals—that is, until the breeding clone gets too old and is sent to slaughter, suggests Lawler. These animals will be used to breed so we will actually eat the offspring of clones. In theory, cloned meat could be raised using organic methods. But ``the USDA has ruled that meat and dairy products from cloned animals and their offspring cannot carry the organic label," says Lawler.[9]

The issue becomes one of ethics. Though the FDA studies of cloned meat found it perfectly safe, it is still a turnoff. At least, this is what the Pew Initiative survey results suggest. People are just uncomfortable with the idea of cloned meat. Andrew Weil, M.D., a natural health adviser, pointed out to Lawler that cloned meat ``is part of an unhealthy trend in food production."[10] Cloned meat—even the offspring of cloned animals—would likely come from factory farms. These farms use hormones and threaten the environment. Cloning would also decrease genetic diversity.

Cloning meat is seen as a way to produce more meat quickly. If we ate only the meat, fish, or poultry necessary to get our required daily amount of protein, the need for cloned meat would not be an issue. The average teen requires only 40 to 50 grams of protein per day.[11] Most Americans get far more protein than this daily due to a diet high in meat and dairy products. While athletes and those with physically demanding jobs need more than 60 grams of protein per day, most of us do not need an 8-ounce steak for dinner. Two cups of milk plus 4 ounces of fish, poultry, or meat provides about 50 grams of protein.

these foods to be labeled. However, organic foods are not allowed to be genetically modified.

But smart breeding is a new technique. According to science writer Anastasia Masurat, it can "radically improve crops without inserting genes from other organisms."[12] It promises to outdo GM because the science has moved on, says Masurat. GM causes fears about food safety and corporations controlling seed stock.

Smart breeding blends the past and the future. It applies the age-old method of crossbreeding with technology. Precise genetic mapping is used to find two varieties to crossbreed. Smart breeding selects specific traits, such as drought resistance, a certain color, or a specific taste. "The dormant genes for many desired traits have been found hiding in rare or wild varieties of some plants. Smart breeders employ crossbreeding techniques to draw out these traits," Masurat explains.[13]

Farmers have been crossbreeding plants and animals for hundreds of years. Perhaps even longer. They learned to breed the strongest to ensure hardy stock or plants that produced more. Sometimes good outcomes arose out of simple luck, and new varieties of plants were the result. Now, scientists are able to use precise information about the plant. They can look to the role each gene plays in a plant's makeup. Crossbreeding can take years. This was one of the reasons that Borlaug came up with shuttle-breeding—to speed up the process. But in

You Can: Feed the Hungry in Your Community

The Green Revolution set out to feed the world. The New Green Revolution seeks ways to rely on renewable resources. You can be a renewable resource in your community, too. Organizations that feed the hungry are always in need of donations. You can do more than donate money or food, though. You can give back to your community by volunteering to work at a soup kitchen or homeless shelter.

Your task as a volunteer might be to make or serve food. It may also be helping with food drives. Find soup kitchens and homeless shelters in your local yellow pages.

Another way is raising money for these organizations. Second Harvest is a group that raises money for organizations in the United States. It focuses solely on feeding those who are starving in this country. A similar program is Hunger Day. You can learn how both programs work by searching for the groups online, then visiting their Web sites.

a lab, smart breeding can speed up the results. "Without genetic modification's expense, patent politics, or potential environmental risks, smart breeding is the best of both worlds," explains Masurat.[14]

A lot can be done with smart breeding techniques. A lot has already been done. Researchers in West Africa created rice that resists disease and drought. American scientists are working on corn plants that turn red when they need water. It is hoped that these new crops will solve hunger and nutrition problems throughout the world.

They are dubbed "superorganics." According to Masurat, "ideally they'll be tasty and safe and won't need as much pesticide, fertilizer, and water."[15] They will please everyone—those who eat them, those who grow them, and those who monitor our food and its impact on the environment.

These smart foods, or superoganics, might be the future of sustainable farming. It builds on the changes farmers are making to ensure that the land can sustain feeding the world for generations. It draws from the success of the first Green Revolution and moves the New Green Revolution into the future. But it is still only part of the cycle for sustainable farming. There are other parts that fit into the cycle, including those who eat the food.

7

Being Truly "Green"

Getting food from field to fork involves many steps. These steps are each a part in the food system. Those who eat the food also have a part in this system. The food system includes those who grow the food, those who ship it, those who sell it, those who package and prepare it, those who buy it, and those who eat it. If you care what goes into your body, you will take an active role in this food system. We are each more powerful than we realize. The money used to buy food provides an advantage. When and where do you spend money on food—supermarkets, farmers' markets, or community gardens? These all act as a vote—for or against—how food is grown and gets to us.

"Green" Teens

Imagine heading to camp for the summer. But at this camp you grow and eat organic vegetables and brew biodiesel fuel. You might also build a habitat to help save threatened wildlife. Some of the teens at this camp choose to teach programs that share eco-friendly living tips with area children. It is a summer camp, so the typical camp activities are part of the program, too. Plan on going horseback riding, swimming, hiking, and rock climbing.

Longacre Farm is a 225-acre organic farm in Newport, Pennsylvania. Solar panels provide energy, and the teens who go to the camp learn to become stewards of the earth. After their summer experiences they leave with new understanding about "the world's ecological balance, and green alternatives to implement back at home and in their classrooms," says Susan Smith, director of the Longacre Leadership Program. A total of seventy-two young people aged twelve to eighteen attended this international program in 2007.[1]

This is one way to explore sustainable living. A new career also focuses on it. EcoGastronomy is a major launched by the University of New Hampshire. Students combine the EcoGastronomy major with nutritional science courses in this degree program. "We are seeing growing student interest in food and sustainability and an eagerness to understand and connect with the local, regional and global food system," says Joanne Curran-Celentrano, professor of nutritional sciences at the University of New Hampshire and cofounder of the program.[2] Students learn how to grow and prepare foods. They work on solutions to the challenges of growing food. Social justice in the food system is another issue they explore. They get experience working at the organic research farm and working with Local Harvest in the university's dining service. Many want to be chefs or caterers or go into the hospitality industry.

The Challenge for Organics
. . . .

Sustainable farming seeks to find a middle ground between growing food on factory and organic farms. The expense of qualifying for an organic rating and the smaller scale of many organic farms means the cost is passed along to the consumer. Should we have to choose between affordable food grown with pesticides and the cost of foods grown without them? This is the challenge for organics. "If organic food is available only to those who can afford to pay a premium for it, then what good can it ultimately do for the planet and its people?" asks Leif Utne, associate editor of *Utne* magazine.[3] The answer is in thinking of food grown without chemicals and pesticides "not as an exclusive luxury but as a basic human right."[4] When the question was asked of Anuradha Mittal, an expert on the politics of food, she outlined ideas for making healthier foods available to low-income people.

Leif Utne summaries the steps necessary:

First, farmers' markets and community-supported agriculture (CSA) farms should all accept food stamps and coupons. . . . A second step would be establishing volunteer programs that would allow low-income people to trade farmwork for food. Inner-city neighborhoods should have their own farmers' markets and even their own farms.

Mittal would like to see more urban farms and vegetable gardens established at schools and other places.

"Thinking about organic food just as a consumer is not enough," she concludes. "We have to be concerned with who grows the food, who gets to eat it, and how many miles it travels."[5]

Food miles are becoming more important. These are the number of miles that food travels from field to table. While food labels provide information on what is in the food and how much nutrition it has, some people want more information. According to food writer Natalie Coomber, "consumers are now asking for . . . where the product was farmed, the food miles it has racked up and whether the food was produced in an organic way."[6] Some supermarkets include signs in the produce section stating where the food was grown. The sources change depending on season. This is one reason why adding food miles to the packages would be very costly. That cost would be passed along to the consumer.

Fuel in the Food System

Whether to buy organic or food that is grown on conventional farms is one debate. Another is whether to use the convenience of a grocery or buy locally. Organic foods are free of pesticides and chemicals. Both require mountains of energy. They also contaminate groundwater and soil. But even organic food can be shipped

Many people are becoming more and more interested in their food. They want to know how it's grown, where it's grown, and how it got to their table.

long distances. According to environmental writer Christie Matheson, "Given that food travels on average of 1,500 miles before it lands on your plate, eating locally has the edge when it comes to using less transportation energy."[7]

Whether food is grown using organic or conventional methods, it is common to ship it not only across the country but across borders. Some is shipped overseas. "In 2005, more than $120 billion of agricultural products crossed U.S. borders as imports and exports," states the Sustainable Table Web site.[8]

This is not good because of the energy used to ship it. Fuel has a big impact on food at nearly every stage. Fuel is used to grow the food we eat. According to the SARE program, a majority of energy used in farming comes from using fertilizers, herbicides, pesticides, and other chemicals. Many are derived from fossil fuel or fuel processing. "Reducing the use of these materials, especially nitrogen fertilizer, is an effective way to cut back energy use on the farm," SARE says. If a farmer used manure instead of nitrogen, he would save around $85 per acre. More significantly, he would save 40,000 cubic feet of natural gas.[9] When less fuel is used, it pollutes the air and water less, too.

One major concern with the food system is specialized farms. Crops, which need fertilizer, are grown miles away from ranches and meat producers. Raising animals for meat requires grain and high-protein feed. But the farms that produce it are miles from the ranches. The livestock generates huge quantities of manure. But there are no fields to spread it on. It could be shipped to crop land, but it is very heavy. It would burn a lot of fuel to get it there. So, it becomes a pollutant. Farmers growing crops end up using chemical fertilizers instead. "As much as forty percent of energy used in the food system goes towards the production of artificial fertilizers and pesticides," states the Sustainable Table Web site.[10]

Farmers and ranchers are finding ways to cut back on fuel use. The SARE program has helped. Different farming methods require less fuel. But farmers are finding alternatives, too. They are using clean energy. Fruit left after harvest is collected and distilled. This creates clean-burning, high-octane fuel to run farm equipment. Some farmers are growing crops just to use in making their own fuel. Corn ethanol is an example. Others use animal waste, according to SARE.[11] Selling surplus fuel is a source of added income for some farm families.

Other efforts to streamline farm production also boost profit by saving money. For example, through the SARE program, farmers are using solar panels to heat greenhouses. They are also replacing old light bulbs with energy-efficient ones. Still other farmers are harnessing wind energy and using improved irrigation methods. These are all sources of clean energy and solutions for streamlining farm production.

Urban Farms

As people become more aware of how food is grown and packaged, many seek alternatives. But those choices are limited in urban areas. There is little space to grow your own food. And getting fresh food other ways is difficult. At least until recently.

A new type of farming is emerging. It is happening in urban areas. So it is called urban farming. The city of Albuquerque, New Mexico, is an example of urban farming. It has been a part of life in Albuquerque for a long time. Dan Schuster, who manages Rio Grande Community Farms, told journalist Heather Clark, "We're so far behind, we're ahead!" As the rest of the country built up, people in Albuquerque continued growing their own food. "The rural lifestyle of backyard horse stables, fresh eggs for breakfast, fruit trees and vegetable gardens that people take for granted in many Albuquerque neighborhoods is catching on around the country," states Clark.[12]

It is catching on in other cities. Urban Farming, a non-profit group in Detroit, Michigan, turns vacant lots into gardens. The group started with three gardens in 2005 and had six hundred three years later. They

A zucchini plant. Many people are starting to grow their own food, even in urban areas.

have since expanded into cities such as New York, St. Louis, Chicago, Atlanta, Minneapolis, and New Orleans, according to Clark.

The urban farm doesn't stop with community gardens, explains Clark. Farmers had often brought organic produce into farmers' markets, restaurants, and schools so people could taste the difference to what they usually ate. Now, local farmers who use commercial farming practices, are "choosing to plant vegetables based on nutritional value and taste, rather than making decisions based on a business contract or how long a vegetable can sit on a shelf," says Clark.[13]

You Can: Do Your Part

You can do something else: compost. Even if you do not have a garden, you can help someone who does. Or, you can donate your compost to a community or church garden. It limits the fuel used to haul away your garbage. And it does something useful with the scraps of food you have not eaten.

Compost is like "black gold." It is the key to organic gardening. Rich soil is very important to farmers and gardeners. Compost is very rich in nutrients from the foods used to make it. It improves soil because it serves as plant food and absorbs moisture.

Writer Abbie Barrett says that quality compost is made of three parts "brown" matter to one part "green" matter.[14] Brown matter includes autumn leaves, hay, and newspaper. Green matter includes lawn clippings, kitchen scraps, algae, and cow manure.

Natural organisms in these things begin to break down whatever is in the compost pile. The scraps decay. This is why it is important to follow the three-part to one-part formula. Otherwise, it will not break down properly. "These organisms play a vital role in your garden by converting your soil's nutrients into a form plants can use, while enticing larger beneficial organisms, like earthworms and spiders, to further enrich the dirt," says Barrett.[15]

When the farmer—whether using commercial, organic, or sustainable farming methods—sells his harvest locally, it reduces fuel use. A portion of the crop does not need to be shipped a long distance. When consumers are able to find a variety of fresh food locally, it is easier to commit to the cycle of sustainable food.

The Cycle of Sustainable Food

Sustainability is not a job only for farmers. Those of us who eat the food have a responsibility, too. To be truly "green" you need to think about how land, water, and air work together. Pollution of soil, water, and air affect plants. How much water is available is also a factor. During times of drought, water use is restricted. When people do not adhere to those restrictions, it further limits water available for farming.

Food-packaging plants use a lot of water and fuel to make easy-to-prepare foods. About a quarter of the energy needed to get food from field to table is used in food processing and packaging, according to the Sustainable Table Web site. Once food is processed it must be heated or cooked at home. This uses even more energy. You can help cut this use by avoiding processed foods. Buy fresh food. Chose foods with less packaging. Cutting back on meat also helps. "Meat is the least fuel-efficient food we have," states the Sustainable Table Web site.[16]

We may at first find it difficult to have to think so much about the food we eat. What does it contain? What do we know about that food? How was it grown? We may miss the convenience of old ways—berries available all year long instead of only during summer, and plenty of choices from globally available food. But knowledge about that food and how it was grown and processed may cancel out the ease of buying it. "Change for the better is seldom easy, but always worth it," says Jim Goodman.[17]

Growing enough food to feed the world is a big responsibility. It requires farmers to become stewards of the earth so that the soil and land will still be able to grow or raise enough food to feed people years from now. But farmers need the commitment of everyone who eats the food, too. We must all work together.

To be a steward of the earth you first need to become a steward of your body. Change begins with choices. Understand what your body needs to be healthy. Select foods that support your body, such as eating more whole, fresh foods that will benefit you. This is easier to do when you support local farmers or food co-ops. Finally, reach out in your community to make sure the hungry are fed. You can do something now through these small choices. Become a steward of your own health and that of the earth by thinking about where your food came from and how it will benefit you.

Chapter Notes

Introduction: **Teens Choosing "Green" Food**

1. Timothy B. Wheeler, "Lake Clifton greenhouse project harvest 1st crops," *Baltimore Sun,* December 17, 2009, <http://www.baltimoresun.com/features/green/bal-md.gr.hoophouse17dec17,0,601643.story> (March 3, 2010).

Chapter 1: **Food, Glorious Food**

1. Institute of Medicine, "Overview of the IOM Report on *Food Marketing to Children and Youth: Threat or Opportunity?*" Fact Sheet, December 2005, <www.iom.edu> (October 3, 2008).
2. "About BMI for Children and Teens," n.d., Centers for Disease Control and Prevention, n.d., <http://www.cdc.gov/healthyweight/assessing/bmi/childrens_BMI/about.htm> (March 3, 2010).
3. National Center for Health Statistics, "Prevalence of overweight among children and adolescents, United States 2003-04," Centers for Disease Control Web site, April 2006, <http://www.cdc.gov/nchs/products/pubs/pubd/hestats/overweight/overwght_child_03.htm> (September 12, 2008).
4. Canadian Institutes of Health Research, "Researchers doing their homework on childhood obesity," August 25, 2005, <http://www.cihr-irsc.gc.ca/e/28857.html> (September 12, 2008).
5. Steven Dowshen, MD, "Metabolism: A Body Basics Article," Kidshealth Web site, p. 2, n.d., <http://kidshealth.org/parent/general/body_basics/metabolism.html> (October 2, 2008).
6. Cheryl Redmond, "Eat Your Vitamins," *Body + Soul* magazine, August 2008, p. 88.
7. Katie Arnold, "The Future Is Green," *Body + Soul* magazine, April 2008, p. 110.
8. Ann Burgess and Peter Glasauer, *Family Nutrition Guide.* Rome, Italy: Food and Agriculture Organization of the United Nations, 2004, p. 14.
9. Jim Goodman, "We Need to Eat Locally Again," The Cornucopia Institute, August 4, 2008, <www.cornucopia.org/2008/08/we-need-to-eat-locally-again> (July 15, 2010).
10. Redmond.

Chapter 2: **From Field to Fork**

1. Eric Schlosser, *Fast Food Nation,* New York: Houghton Mifflin Company. 2001, p. 173.
2. "Slaughterhouses and processing," Sustainable Table Web site, September 2009, <http://www.sustainabletable.org/issues/processing/> (April 10, 2009).
3. Ibid.
4. "Food Additives," FDA/IFIC Brochure, U.S. Food and Drug Administration, p. 5 of 7, January 1992, <http://www.foodsafety.gov/~lrd/foodaddi.html> (February 1, 2009).
5. Nutrient Data Laboratory, USDA Table of Nutrient Retention Factors, Release 6. U.S. Department of Agriculture, Agricultural Research Service, Beltsville Human Nutrition Research Center, Maryland, December 2007, <http://www.ars.usda.gov/Services/docs.htm?docid-8964> (February 23, 2010) and "Nutritional Effects of Food Processing: Freezing, Drying, Cooking, and Reheating," n.d., <http://www.nutritiondata.com/> (February 22, 2009).
6. "About the Food and Drug Administration," U.S. Food and Drug Administration, June 18, 2009, <http://www.fda.gov/AboutFDA/WhatWeDo/WhatFDADoesn'tRegulate/default.htm> (February 5, 2010).
7. "Food Additives."
8. Judith E. Foulke, "A Fresh Look at Food Preservatives," *FDA Consumer*, U. S. Food and Drug Administration, October 1993, <http://www.cfsan.fda.gov/~dms/fdpreser.html> (February 1, 2009).
9. "Food Ingredients Backgrounder." 2007-2009 IFIC Foundation Media Guide on Food Safety and Nutrition, n.d., <http://ific.org> (October 10, 2008).
10. Lynne Olver, "Food Timeline FAQs: Mesopotamia through Shakespeare," Food Timeline Web site, July 12, 2009, <http://www.foodtimeline.org/foodfaq3.html#egypt> (February 18, 2010).
11. Marshall Brain, "How Food Preservation Works," How Stuff Works, October 30, 2008, <http://recipes.howstuffworks.com/food-preservation.htm> (February 22, 2009).
12. Ibid., p. 2.
13. Charlotte P. Brennard, PhD, "Ten Most Commonly Asked Questions About Food Irradiation Food Fact Safety Sheet" March 1995 FN-250.8, Idaho State University Radiation Information Network's Food Irradiation Web site, <http://www.physics.isu.edu/radinf/food.htm> (February 23, 2010).
14. Brain, p. 2.

Chapter 3: **The Business of Growing Food**

1. Daniel R. Ess, "Ag101: Demographics," Agriculture Web site of U.S. Environmental Protection Agency, Purdue Research Foundation. September 11, 2007, <http://www.epa.gov/oecaagct/ag101/demographics.html> (January 15, 2009).

2. Jim Goodman, "We Need to Eat Locally Again," The Cornucopia Institute, August 4, 2008, <www.cornucopia.org/2008/08/we-need-to-eat-locally-again> (July 15, 2010).

3. James E. Horne, PhD, and Maura McDermott, *The Next Green Revolution: Essential Steps to a Healthy, Sustainable Agriculture.* New York: Good Products Press/Hawthorn Press, 2001, p. 10.

4. Jane Frankenberger, "Ag101: Crop Production," Agriculture Web site of U.S. Environmental Protection Agency, Purdue Research Foundation, September 11, 2007, <http://www.epa.gov/oecaagct/ag101/crop.html> (March 28, 2009).

5. "Fossil Fuel and Energy Use," Sustainable Table Web site, n.d., <http://www.sustainabletable.org/issues/energy/index_pf.html> (February 7, 2009).

6. "Ethylene Facts," from Catalytic Generators Web site, n.d., <http://www.catalyticgenerators.com/whatisethylene.html> (October 3, 2008).

7. "Label Lowdown: Cruelty Free," in Whole Living, *Body + Soul* magazine, September 2008, p. 28

8. Don G. Jones, "Ag101: Pork Production," Agriculture Web site of U.S. Environmental Protection Agency, Purdue Research Foundation, September 10, 2008, <http://www.epa.gov/oecaagct/ag101/pork.html> (April 10, 2009).

9. David Harvey, "Poultry and Eggs: Background," April 16, 2009, USDA Economic Research Service, April 16, 2009, <http://www.ers.usda.gov/Briefing/Poultry/Background.htm> (March 4, 2010).

10. U.S. Broiler Industry: Background Statistics and Information, May 5, 2009, <http://www.ers.usda.gov/News/broilercoverage.htm> (March 3, 2010).

11. Tom Applegate, "Ag101: Poultry Production," Agriculture Web site of U.S. Environmental Protection Agency, Purdue Research Foundation, September 10, 2009, <www.epa/gov/oecaagct/ag101/poultry.html> (April 10, 2009).

12. Horne, p. 43.

13. Ibid., pp. 42-56

14. Bryan A. McCarty, "Local vs Organic Conundrum," *Keep Green Going,* from Environmental News Network, March 21, 2008, <http://www.enn.com> (September 2, 2008).

15. Lisa Roberts, "The Good and Bad about Organics," *Orlando Sentinel,* from Environmental News Network, February 22, 2006, <http://www.enn.com> (September 2, 2008).
16. Libby Quaid, "Parents Worried about Pesticides Turn to Organic Food," Associated Press, November 3, 2005, from Environmental News Network, <http://www.enn.com> (September 2, 2008).
17. Roberts.
18. Christie Matheson, "The world's best diet," *Body + Soul* magazine, June 2008, p. 98.
19. Michael Pollan, "Back to the Heart of Organics," *Utne*, September-October 2004, p. 92.
20. Ibid.
21. "Community Supported Agriculture," Alternative Farming Systems Information Center Web site, December 7, 2009, <http://www.nal .usda.gov/afsic/pubs/csa/csa.shtml> (February 27, 2010).
22. Pollan, p. 94.
23. Ibid.
24. Ibid.
25. Ibid.
26. Ibid.

Chapter 4: **The Green Revolution**

1. James E. Horne, PhD, and Maura McDermott. *The Next Green Revolution: Essential Steps to a Healthy, Sustainable Agriculture.* New York: Good Products Press/Hawthorn Press, 2001, pp. 15-16.
2. Leon Hesser, *The Man Who Fed the World: An Authorized Biography of Nobel Peace Prize Laureate Norman Borlaug and His Battle to End World Hunger.* Dallas, Tex: Durban House Publishing, 2006, p. 61.
3. Ibid., p. 42.
4. Ibid., p. 41.
5. Ibid., p. 54.
6. Ibid., p. 41.
7. Ibid., p. 57.
8. "Helping Hungry Families Feed Themselves," , Heifer International, n.d., <http://www.heifer.org> (November 12, 2008).
9. Terry L. Anderson and Bruce Yandle, editors, *Agriculture and the Environment: Searching for Greener Pastures.* Stanford, Calif.: Stanford University/Hoover Institution Press, 2001.
10. Horne, p. 16.

11. Jim Goodman, "We Need to Eat Locally Again," The Cornucopia Institute, August 4, 2008, < www.cornucopia.org/2008/08/we-need-to-eat-locally-again> (July 15, 2010).

12. "FDA Releases Final Guidance on Genetically Engineered Animals," U.S. Food and Drug Administration, January 15, 2009, <http://www.fda/gov/ForConsumers/ConsumerUpdates/ucm092738.htm> (February 13, 2010).

13. "Genetically Modified Foods," Healthline, n.d., <http://www.healthline.com/adamcontent/genetically-engineered-foods.htm> (February 22, 2009).

14. Goodman, p. 2.

Chapter 5: Food Security

1. James E. Horne, PhD, and Maura McDermott. *The Next Green Revolution: Essential Steps to a Healthy, Sustainable Agriculture.* New York: Good Products Press/Hawthorn Press, 2001, p. 9.

2. Ibid.

3. Ibid,, p. 10.

4. Ibid.

5. Ibid,, p. 11.

6. Ibid,, p. 10.

7. Jim Goodman, "We Need to Eat Locally Again," The Cornucopia Institute, August 4, 2008, < www.cornucopia.org/2008/08/we-need-to-eat-locally-again> (July 15, 2010).

8. Elizabeth Weise, "Soil Program Reaps World Food Prize," *USA Today,* October 24, 2002, 10d.

9. Ibid.

10. Ibid.

11. Ibid.

12. Dara Moskowitz, "Beyond Organics–to Bliss: Want really natural eating? Try the taste of terroir," Utne, September-October 2004, p. 98.

13. Ibid., p. 97.

14. Ibid.

15. Ibid.

16. Horne, p. 11.

17. David Mackay, "How Drought Is Parching the World's Food Industry." Foodprocessing Technology, September 29, 2008, <http://www.foodprocessing-technology.com/features/feature42194/> (February 22, 2009).

18. Ibid., p. 2 of 3.

19. Ibid.

20. The Vegetarian Resource Group. "Types of Vegetarians," n.d., <http://www.vrg.org/nutshell/faq.htm> (March 1, 2010).

21. "A Healthy Way to Live," n.d., <http:://www.veganoutreach.org> (January 12, 2009).
22. Reed Mangels, PhD, "Vegetarian Nutrition for Teenagers," The Vegetarian Resource Group, 2007 Pamphlet, p. 2.
23. The Vegetarian Resource Group, " Vegan Diets in a Nutshell," n.d., <http://www.vrg.org/nutshell/faq.htm> (March 1, 2010).
24. Horne, p. 16.
25. Ibid
26. Ibid., p. 17.
27. Ibid., p. 16.
28. Ibid., p. 17.
29. "How Much Protein Do You Really Need?" Healthy U: Your Pathway to Wellness, Northwestern Health Sciences University, n.d., < http://www.nwhealth.edu/healthyU/eatWell/protein_2.html> (July 15, 2010).
30. Pollan, p. 92.

Chapter 6: **The New Green Revolution**

 1. "Exploring Sustainability in Agriculture," Opportunities in Agriculture Bulletin, Sustainable Agriculture and Research Education, n.d., <http://www.sare.org/publications/explore/index .htm> (September 27, 2008).
 2. James E. Horne, PhD, and Maura McDermott. *The Next Green Revolution: Essential Steps to a Healthy, Sustainable Agriculture.* New York: Good Products Press/Hawthorn Press, 2001, p. 37.
 3. Ibid., p. 35.
 4. "Exploring Sustainability in Agriculture," Opportunities in Agriculture Bulletin, Sustainable Agriculture and Research Education, n.d., <http://www.sare.org/publications/explore/index .htm> (September 27, 2008).
 5. Horne, p. 55.
 6. Andrew Lawler, "The Clone Wars," *Body + Soul* magazine, June 2008, p.72.
 7. Ibid.
 8. Ibid., p. 70.
 9. Ibid., p. 72.
10. Ibid.
11. "Protein: A Guide for Teens" at Young Women's Health Web site. March 17, 2009, <http://www.youngwomenshealth.org/protein .htm> (March 1, 2010).
12. Anastasia Masurat, "The Future of Farming: Outsmarting GM." *The Utne Reader*, September/October, 2004, p. 100.
13. Ibid.

14. Ibid.
15. Ibid.

Chapter 7: **Being Truly "Green"**

1. "Green + Teen = Enriching Summer," Longacre Farm press release, January 14, 2008.
2. Lori Wright, "University of New Hampshire Launches Groundbreaking EcoGastronomy Program: First-of-its-kind program educates students about sustainable food systems," from Industry News at *Hospitality Net, September 2, 2008,* <http://www .hospitalitynet.org> (September 2, 2008).
3. Leif Utne, "Can Organics Feed the Masses?" *Utne,* September-October 2004, pp. 98–99.
4. Ibid.
5. Ibid.
6. Natalie Coomber, "Sustainable Food Production from Farm to Fork." Foodprocessing Technology, November 14, 2008, <http://www .foodprocessing-technology.com/features/feature45625/> (February 22, 2009).
7. Christie Matheson, "The world's best diet," *Body + Soul* magazine, June 2008, p. 97.
8. "Fossil Fuel and Energy Use," Sustainable Table Web site, n.d., <http://www.sustainabletable.org/issues/energy/index_pf.html> (February 7, 2009).
9. "Clean Energy Farming," Opportunities in Agriculture Bulletin, Sustainable Agriculture Research and Education, n.d.,<http://www .sare.org/publications/energy/index.shtml> (September 27, 2008).
10. Sustainable Table.
11. SARE.
12. Heather Clark, "Urban Farms Grow as Cities Seek Safe, Cheap Food," *Ag News*, September 2, 2008, <http://www.agweekly.com> (September 6, 2008).
13. Ibid.
14. Abbie Barrett, "Beginners Guide to Organic Gardening," *Body + Soul* magazine, May 2008, pp. 115-121.
15. Ibid.
16. Sustainable Table.
17. Jim Goodman, "Farmer Markets: Think Local as Well as Organic," Organic Consumers Association, from Environmental News Network, July 25, 2008, <http://www.enn.com> (September 2, 2008).

Glossary

artificial—Not from nature; man-made or created in a laboratory.

conventional—The usual way to do something; following a traditional pattern.

crossbreeding—Interbreeding or blending elements of two different plants or animals.

DNA—Deoxyribonucleic acid; a substance present in the center of almost every cell in every living thing that contains genetic information.

ethylene—A hormone that speeds the sequences of growth, development, ripening, and aging in plants; also, a byproduct of propane, diesel, and gasoline powered engines.

factory farm—A very large farm owned by a company and run like a factory to limit costs and increase profit.

fertilizer—Either a chemical or natural material, such as manure, added to soil to increase growth of plants.

genetic modification (GM)—Changing a plant or animal's structure by removing DNA and replacing it with that of another plant or animal.

high-yield crops—Crops bred for larger than normal harvest.

hybrid—The offspring of two different varieties of plants or animals; something made by combining different elements.

industrial farming—Large farms using large equipment to produce more food.

macronutrients—Nutrient needed by the body in large amounts, such as proteins and carbohydrates.

micronutrients—Nutrients needed by the body in small amounts, such as vitamins and minerals.

microorganism—A microscopic living thing, such as a virus, fungus, or bacterium.

monoculture—Crops of a single type of plant; growing the same crop in the same plot of land year after year.

natural—Coming from nature; not made, treated, or changed by humans.

nitrogen—A chemical element that makes up about 78 percent of the earth's atmosphere.

nutrition—The act of taking in nourishment that the body uses for growth and life.

organic—Coming from living matter; not grown or produced with chemicals or man-made fertilizers.

pesticide—A substance used to kill insects and other pests.

phosphorus—A natural mineral used to fertilize crops.

processing—A series of steps to change food for packing or to treat food to preserve it.

production—The action of making or processing something.

residue—The part of a plant left after harvest. The roots and stem or stalk on top of the soil; a film or small amount of something left after washing.

shuttle-breeding—Sending seeds back and forth between two plots of land for planting so new seeds can be used in crossbreeding. This speeds up the development of new plant varieties.

sustainable—Able to be kept up or maintained.

synthetic—Artificial; man-made.

Further Reading

Baines, John. *Food for Life.* North Mankato, Minn.: Smart Apple Media, 2007.

Ballard, Carol. *Sustainable Food Production.* Mankato, Minn.: Arcturus Publishing, 2010.

Barker, Geoff. *Hunger.* Mankato, Minn.: Smart Apple Media, 2010.

Kidd, J.S., and Renee A. Kidd. *Agricultural Versus Environmental Science: A Green Revolution.* New York: Chelsea House Publishers, 2006.

Mason, Paul. *How Big Is Your Food Footprint?* New York: Marshall Cavendish Benchmark, 2009.

Reynolds, Jan. *Cycle of Rice, Cycle of Life: A Story of Sustainable Farming.* New York: Lee & Low Books, 2009.

Internet Addresses

The Green Guide
    \<http://thegreenguide.com\>

Nutrition.gov: Smart Nutrition Starts Here
    \<http://www.nutrition.gov/\>

SARE (Sustainable Agriculture Research and Education)
    \<http://www.sare.org/\>

Index